W9-BSY-165

ALSO BY REINHOLD MESSNER

All 14 Eight Thousanders

Everest: Expedition to the Ultimate

To the Top of the World:
Alpine Challenges in the Himalaya and Karakoram

The Crystal Horizon: Everest—The First Solo Ascent

Reinhold Messner, Free Spirit: A Climber's Life

Antarctica: Both Heaven and Hell

Big Walls: History, Routes, Experiences

The Challenge

K2

The Seventh Grade: Most Extreme Climbing

Solo: Nanga Parbat

MY QUEST FOR THE YETI

THE YETI

CONFRONTING

THE HIMALAYAS' DEEPEST

MYSTERY

Reinhold Messner

TRANSLATED BY PETER CONSTANTINE

ST. MARTIN'S PRESS ✠ NEW YORK

The excerpt from *The Long Walk* by Slavomir Rawicz is reprinted with permission from The Lyons Press.

Library of Congress Cataloging-in-Publication Data

Messner, Reinhold.
    [Yeti—Legende und Wirklichkeit. English]
    My quest for the yeti : confronting the Himalayas' deepest mystery / Reinhold Messner; translated by Peter Constantine.—1st ed.
        p. cm.
    Includes bibliographical references.
    ISBN 0-312-20394-2
    1. Yeti.   2. Messner, Reinhold, 1944—Journeys—Himalaya Mountains Region. I. Title.
    QL89.2.Y4M4713   2000
    001.944—dc21   99-055091

Book design by Kate Nichols

First published in Germany under the title *Yeti:
Legende und Wirklichkeit* by S. Fisher Verlag

First Edition: April 2000

1   3   5   7   9   10   8   6   4   2

WHAT APPEARS AS A MONSTER

WHAT IS CALLED A MONSTER

WHAT IS RECOGNIZED AS A MONSTER

EXISTS WITHIN A HUMAN BEING HIMSELF

AND DISAPPEARS WITH HIM

—MILAREPA, SHERPA POET (A.D. 1040–1123)

NOTE TO THE READER

I have tried throughout this book to be as faithful as possible to the meanings and pronunciations of the Chinese, Tibetan, and other native Himalayan words I encountered on my journeys. However, because of the vagaries of dialects, concrete, word-for-word translations for the yeti are as elusive as the creature itself. Despite their impressionistic nature, I hope the following partial list of rough translations and tentative etymologies (citing romanized versions of either written Tibetan forms or standard Chinese pronunciations) will prove useful to the reader. For further reading I recommend *Languages and Dialects of Tibeto-Burman* by James A. Matisoff with Stephen P. Baron and John B. Lowe, IAS Publications: University of California, 1996. Many thanks to Professor Julian Wheatley of MIT for his help.

beshung: Chinese, "bai xiong"—"white bear."

dzu teh, tshute, tsetu: spoken Tibetan, "tse-t'u"—"child of chemo."

dremo/dremong/chemo/chemong: cf. written Tibetan, "dred"—"bear"; "dredmo"—"female bear."

mashiung: Chinese, "maxiong"—"brown bear."

migyu, migo, mygio, migiv: cf. written Tibetan, "mi"—"person"; "man" and "wild."

renshung: Chinese, "ren xiong"—"man bear."

thelma: spoken Tibetan, "the-moh" or "telmoh"—"monkey."

tom: written Tibetan, "dom"—"bear."

CONTENTS

Note to Reader   ix

Map   xii

Yeti Research Expeditions   xv

1. July 1986: Somewhere in Tibet   1

2. Reunited in Lhasa   19

3. Confusion in Katmandu   33

4. Tales of the Yeti   57

5. Gods and Demons   71

6. Among the Yak Nomads   83

7. Curiosity and Ridicule   91

8. "Glacial Cosmogony" and "Ancestral Legacy"   107

9. Footprints in the Snow   123

10. White Head and Black Giant   135

11. The Pieces Fit   149

12. Life and Legend   159

Notes   167

Works Mentioned in the Text   169

YETI RESEARCH

EXPEDITIONS

1970–85: Thirty Expeditions to the Himalayas and the Karakorum Mountains.

Summer 1985: Travels from Lhasa to the holy Kailash Mountain; treks through parts of the Chang Tang, a frozen desert between the Trans-Himalayas and the Kunlun Mountains.

Winter 1986: Expedition to Makalu.

Summer 1986: In Kham (formally in eastern Tibet), after an adventurous three-thousand-mile drive, Reinhold Messner treks twelve hundred miles on foot from Tarchen Gompa near Kanze to Lhasa.

August–September 1986: Expedition to Makalu (the valleys of Arun and Barun).

October 1986: Stay at Solo Khumbu in central Nepal.

Summer 1987: Trip to the Hindu Kush.

May 1987: Trek through western Bhutan.

Early summer 1988: Trek through Amdo to Kham and back.

March–April 1989: Solo to Khumbu.

Summer 1989: Trip to the Pamir Mountains.

Early summer 1991: Journey through the length of Bhutan.

December 1992: Trek to Solo Khumbu and Mustang (and back over Manang).

January–March 1993: Trips to Rolwaling and Sikkim.

May 1994: Trip through the Garhwal Himalayas in northern India.

June 1995: Trip to the Altai Mountains in southern Siberia.

Early summer 1996: Trip through eastern Tibet.

Fall 1996: Trip to the holy Kailash Mountain.

May–June 1997: Expedition to the mountains of eastern Tibet.

July 1997: Trip to Kazakhstan (Tien Shan Mountains).

August 1997: Stay in Baltistan.

July 1998: Ursula Schäfer bequeaths Reinhold Messner the head and pelt of a *chemo* for his collection at Schloss Juval. Her husband, the zoologist Ernst Schäfer, had shot the animal in eastern Tibet.

August 1998: Trip to Mongolia.

Postscript:

Fall 1998: Reinhold Messner presents all his yeti material (precise maps, details, addresses) to a team of scientists.

MY QUEST FOR THE YETI

1

The waters of the Mekong River, swollen from the melting snow, had forced me deeper into one of the countless Tibetan valley rifts. There was no choice—I would have to fight my way through the churning waters. I found what looked to be the best spot and waded in. With every step the powerful current threatened to sweep my legs out from under me. After finding a firm foothold and shifting my weight to one leg, I would muster all my strength and lift the other leg. Progress was slow, but eventually I found myself standing in the middle of the raging waters, leaning on a branch braced against the current, trying not to panic. Turning back now was impossible.

The opposite bank, a dark strip stretched between coniferous trees and glistening black rock, was only a stone's throw away. The frigid water was gray as fog, and the spray tasted of rock and dirty

1

snow. I was glad I had kept my boots on. Seven of my toes had been amputated in 1970 after an expedition to Nanga Parbat, the eight-thousand-meter mountain in northern India, and the boots helped me get a stronger foothold between the stones.

Positioning myself for my next step, fixing my eyes on a rock that lay on the opposite bank, I slid my right foot into a gap between two stones beneath the seething waters. The trick was to find my balance and then simply place my trust in the riverbed. I inched my way forward, upstream, diagonally against the current.

The water was so cold that I could not feel my legs below my knees, but my face was covered with sweat. My arms were exhausted from gripping the branch and from flailing to keep my balance. Finally I reached the dark bank, exhausted but exhilarated.

My exact location was difficult to pinpoint. I had come from Qamdo in eastern Tibet and was trying to make my way south to Nachu. I had crossed the valleys of some of Asia's greatest rivers: the Yangtze, the Mekong, and the Salween. The mountain ranges towering over the river valleys were so craggy and steep that people had managed to settle in only a few places. I often trekked for two days without encountering a single soul.

Once you get off the roads in eastern Tibet the mountains become completely impregnable. With a yak caravan or with some sturdy Tibetan ponies you might manage to reach certain locations. Trekking alone and on foot meant sacrificing every comfort. I had a sleeping bag, a flashlight, some bacon and hard bread, a pocketknife, a waterproof cover, and a camera. But no tent. Whenever I couldn't make it to a village by sundown, I slept in the open, in a cave, or under a tree.

Sitting on a dry rock above the riverbank, I took off my shoes, wrung out my socks, and slowly began to warm up a little. The bubbling water now sounded soothing. An incredibly dense forest lay before me. I would need to cross it by sundown, and the sun's rays were already slanting. After putting my wet socks and shoes back on, I heaved my rucksack back onto my shoulders. It seemed much heavier than it had when I crossed the surging glacial waters.

I had not come to Tibet this time to climb a mountain or to cross a desert. Instead, I wanted to follow the route the Sherpa people had taken in their flight from the lands of Dege, across Qamdo, Alando, Lharigo, Lhasa, and Tingri, then all the way to the Khumbu territories—a migration that still echoed through many Sherpa legends though it had occurred centuries ago. By retracing the Sherpas' journey, I hoped to discover how closely the legend corresponded to reality.

Dense rhododendron bushes and barberry thickets made progress almost impossible. The undergrowth was as impenetrable as a tropical rain forest. I tried to remember which direction the natives of the last village had told me to take. One yak herdsman had hinted that following the wrong riverbed could lead one into falling rocks and avalanches.

The forest was silent—not even a breeze stirred the air. White tufts of cloud floated high above the slanting peaks of the conifer trees. In the sky above the gorge, which seemed close enough to touch, a few birds hovered, as if lost.

A little daylight was still left and the weather was good, so I kept climbing. Trekking became easier the deeper I went into the forest. Rocks and tree trunks of centuries-old Himalayan cedars were less daunting than the hydrangeas, woody weeds, clematis, rhododendron, and maple thickets that clogged every trail near the river. I am usually not prone to fear, but on this day I was apprehensive about finding a trail, a clue, some reassurance. Whenever I had to climb a steep rock, I stopped, my arm propped on my knee, trying to catch my breath and calm my racing pulse. Looking down into the ravine reminded me that this was the edge of the world. I could only hope I was heading for the village of Tchagu.

During all the weeks of trekking I had somehow managed to find paths and trails. Sometimes I tagged along with yak caravans. There had always been somebody to tell me what route to take when I set off alone for the next village. But the Alando region, where I had expected to find a settlement, was deserted—not a hut to be seen, not even the crumbling walls of abandoned homes or the remains of campfires, and therefore not a soul to tell me which way to go.

I sat on a moss-covered rock, took a map out of my backpack, and looked at the tangle of red and blue lines between which were a mass of numbers and place names. Trying to pinpoint my exact position on the map was, however, hopeless. Get lost here and nobody will find you. I folded up the map and sat staring into the high mountain world from which I had come. I have been through this before, I told myself. There were times when I had trekked for sixteen hours straight with barely enough food to keep me going.

The sun's rays no longer penetrated the tall trees; it had become so cold that the skin beneath my sweat-drenched shirt tightened. Deep in the ravine, the meltwater, which would soon reach its high point, flowed smoothly. I had to find a settlement by sundown, or at least reach the high pastures beyond the forest.

The peaks in the east shimmered in the fading light of the evening sun. Dusk was spreading over the forest floor. Barely visible through the trees and the underbrush, I saw what looked like a mountain path not ten feet away from where I had been sitting. I began climbing faster, my pace almost mechanical, and emerged from the verdant undergrowth into a clearing. This was unques-tionably a mountain path—the trail I had anxiously been searching for for so long. I followed it without hesitating, making my way up toward where I thought Tchagu must be. My exhilaration grew with every breath.

Then, suddenly, silent as a ghost, something large and dark stepped into a space thirty feet ahead among the rhododendron bushes. A yak, I thought, becoming excited at the thought of meeting some Tibetans and getting a hot meal and a place to sleep that evening. But the thing stood still. Then, noiseless and light-footed, it raced across the forest floor, disappearing, reappearing, picking up speed. Neither branches nor ditches slowed its progress. This was not a yak.

The fast-moving silhouette dashed behind a curtain of leaves and branches, only to step out into a clearing some ten yards away for a few seconds. It moved upright. It was as if my own shadow had been projected onto the thicket. For one heartbeat it stood motionless, then turned away and disappeared into the dusk. I had expected to hear it make some sound, but there was nothing. The forest remained silent: no stones rolled down the slope, no twigs snapped. I might have heard a few soft footfalls in the grayness of the underbrush.

I stared, first amazed, then perplexed, at the spot where this apparition had stood. Why had I not taken a picture? I stood stock-still, listening to the silence, my senses as alert as those of an animal. Then I crept into the undergrowth from which the creature had emerged only to disappear again, noting everything that moved, every sound that rose above the murmur of the lightest breeze, every scent different from that of the forest floor. There in the black clay, I found a gigantic footprint. It was absolutely distinct. Even the toes were unmistakable. To see that the imprint was fresh I touched the soil next to it. It was fresh. I took a picture and checked the soil around it. My shoes didn't sink in nearly as deeply as had the creature's bare soles.

Staring at the black clay, I suddenly remembered the famous photograph of a footprint Eric Shipton had taken in 1951 at the Melung Glacier, located between Tibet and Nepal. This photograph was commonly considered the best proof that the creature known as the yeti existed. Like all Himalaya climbers, I knew the yeti legends well enough. They are told throughout Sherpa country. But I would never have imagined that a real, living creature might be connected to this legend. I knew large parts of Tibet and the Himalayas pretty well, yet even in those remote places where we mountain climbers, with our modern equipment, can survive for months at a time, I had never seen anything resembling such a creature.

The yeti legend drew strength from the drama of the Himalayan landscape—the peaks, glaciers, snowstorms, and howling winter nights. This was a place where storytelling came naturally—and the oral tradition was alive and well. How often in the kitchen tents of the base camps had the Sherpas told me of the yeti—of the girls it had abducted, of the yaks it had killed in a single blow, of the enormous footprints it had left behind in the snow. I had only half listened in the smoky gloom of the tent, crouching between the equipment and the boxes of supplies, as the Sherpas recounted tales of a dangerous giant, paying full attention only when one of them named real place names or spoke of someone who had actually either encountered a yeti or climbed in pursuit of one. But when I asked for specifics, fathers would turn into grandfathers, villages into regions, and definite facts into blurry maybes. My mind would turn to more concrete concerns.

Yeti legends—spreading over the Himalayas and Tibet like the waters that rush down from the mountains in the summer—had trickled into every village, every household. The Sherpas may have brought the legends back with them from Nepal, Sikkim, and Solo Khumbu. Members of the first Western expeditions to the Himalayas had heard them, and they got picked up in newspapers and books. In less than a century, news of a mysterious creature had spread throughout the world. Today millions of people in the West have some notion of the yeti. For most, it embodies a longing for some mirror to our prehistoric past, a mirror into which we can look and shudder in awe and horror. Yeti stories inevitably boost sales of newspapers and tabloids.

As I continued up the mountain path, looking for tracks, it suddenly struck me that no one on this trip had mentioned the yeti. No one had warned me—seriously or in jest—that something might be afoot in the ravines beneath the mountain peaks. Perhaps the yeti craze had never reached regions where words like *Neanderthal* or *King Kong* were utterly foreign.

That evening I saw four more footprints. The animal was moving up the mountain and climbing farther up into the forest. If it was an animal. Had it been a bear, there would also have been imprints of its forepaws, and the tracks of snow leopards were, I knew, much smaller.

The icy mountain wind blew harder, and the birdsongs high up in the trees became softer and more intermittent. Climbing faster, I could hear nothing but my breathing and the echo of my steps.

The path up to the tree line was arduous, and I was worried that at any moment it would peter out. A gurgling noise came from farther up—whether it came from the ravine through which the river was tumbling or was produced by wind blowing through the treetops that towered into the night I could not tell. By now darkness had fallen. My plan had been to hike till sunset and then bivouac, but the idea of settling down among the roots of a giant cedar to wait for morning did not appeal.

So I pushed on. Sometime between dusk and midnight I came out of the forest into a clearing. Bright moonlight filled the valley before me. Black mountains cast sharp shadows on the slopes. The snaky coils of the mountain trail, which ran over the rises and dips of the pasture, disappeared into the darkness of a moraine. Not a single hut was to be seen. No scent of animals in the air. No dots of light.

Making my way through some ash-colored juniper bushes, I suddenly heard an eerie sound—a whistling noise, similar to the warning call mountain goats make. Out of the corner of my eye I saw the outline of an upright figure dart between the trees to the edge of the clearing, where low-growing thickets covered the steep slope. The figure hurried on, silent and hunched forward, disappearing behind a tree only to reappear again against the moonlight. It stopped for a moment and turned to look at me. Again I heard the whistle, more of an angry hiss, and for a heartbeat I saw eyes and teeth. The creature towered menacingly, its face a gray shadow, its body a black outline. Covered with hair, it stood upright on two short legs and had powerful arms that hung down almost to its knees. I guessed it to be over seven feet tall. Its body looked much heavier than that of a man of that size, but it moved with such agility and power toward the edge of the escarpment that I was both startled and relieved. Mostly I was stunned. No human would have been able to run like that in the middle of the night. It stopped again beyond the trees by the low-growing thickets, as if to catch its breath, and stood motionless in the moonlit night without looking back. I was too mesmerized to take my binoculars out of my backpack.

The longer I stared at it, the more the figure seemed to change shape, but it was similar to whatever it was I had come across farther down the trail—that much I knew. A heavy stench hung in the air, and the creature's receding calls resounded within me. I heard it plunge into the thicket, saw it rush up the slope on all fours, higher and higher, deeper into the night and into the mountains, until it disappeared and all was still again.

I stared into the depths of the night sky. My hands were shaking. The Sherpas used to say that whistling meant danger, and that to escape a yeti one should move downhill as quickly as possible. How could anyone run through the thickets and the underbrush as fast as that creature had? It had disappeared over the moonlight-flecked slopes without stumbling once, as if driven by some monstrous fury.

The thought that my mysterious counterpart might reappear sent chills down my spine. Escaping by fleeing—up or down the mountainside—was clearly futile. I would have broken both legs and made myself into easier prey than I already was. I took out my flashlight and continued up the trail, stopping to listen and look behind me. I felt watched.

The trail ended in a mountain torrent. I longed for a safe place to spend what remained of the night, but crossing the stream in the darkness was impossible. There was no bridge, and from what I could tell, the water would come at least up to my hips. I heard large stones rolling in the torrent and saw silvery white crests. Frost had covered the rocks on the banks of the glacial torrent. I knew the current would only ease in the late morning, before more ice began melting high in the glacier regions. That would be the best time to cross to the other side. I decided to return to the meadow.

Lonely and dead tired, I looked for a place to camp and found some rocks that, over decades, the waters had piled into a natural dam. I didn't have much of a choice. A little farther down the valley I could see a riverbed and hear the water I had crossed late that afternoon.

A metallic sheen lay on the rocks and weeds as I rolled out my thick foam-rubber mat. I constructed a little barrier of rocks between my campsite and the open meadow—a semblance of shelter—and slipped into my sleeping bag. My head propped against my half-empty backpack, I stared into the night sky. Every time I closed my eyes, I imagined the outline of a monster glaring down at me, so I kept them open. The moonlight was visible only on the slopes higher up in a side valley.

I heard the whistling call again. I jumped up. It could not have been the wind. The creature had come back. I peered down into the dark valley, then at the torrent across the slope. I could hear my heartbeat and the hissing and bubbling of the water—or was that the whistle? Had the call come from far away or nearby?

I stuffed my sleeping bag into my backpack and set off up the mountain, following the path along the bank of the stream. Somewhere there had to be a crossing where even at night I could reach the other side.

To my surprise and delight I did find a footbridge. I edged my way over the wooden planks high above the stream, then continued up the opposite slope, snaking my way over stones and boulders to a ridge from which I could see more mountain pastures—and also a few huts. They seemed abandoned; no lights burning anywhere. The village was surrounded by thornbushes and stone barriers and looked eerie and desolate. Piles of firewood stood like sentries in front of the houses. As I approached, I made as much noise as possible. I wanted to be heard. It is dangerous for a stranger to suddenly turn up in a mountain village in the dead of night. He might easily be mistaken for a thief. *Tashi delek!* I called out—first softly, then more loudly. Still nothing stirred. Again I called out *Tashi delek,* the Tibetan greeting. Again nothing. No sound, no light, no sign of life. Was this Tchagu?

Still calling, I walked slowly along a narrow cattle path, peering between the piles of firewood into the forecourts and the low-lying huts behind them. Fear and fury made me call louder. Why did nobody answer?

The only sign of life was the cold stench of horse manure, decay, and urine. Tchagu was no more than a line of derelict huts, a way station without hope—two dozen or so, all of them alike, each with a stone foundation and a wooden saddle roof. Between them darkness yawned. Narrow ladders propped up next to the low doors led to lofts that opened toward the path. The huts looked equally dilapidated. I had no choice but to choose one. Forgetting all my routine precautions, I entered a courtyard through an opening in a pile of firewood and looked for a dry place for the rest of the night.

As I neared the door of the hut, a black mass with snarling teeth and four eyes came flying at me. I grabbed a branch out of the woodpile behind me and retreated back down the path. A Tibetan mastiff. Soon other dogs joined in. I had Tibetan mastiffs back home in Austria. Brown patches next to their eyes make it look as if they have four eyes. These dogs are big and they are dangerous.

I swung the long, thick branch like a club, ready to bludgeon any slavering dog that got too close. I stood with my back to the stone barrier that separated the village from the fields behind it. The ferocious pack was closing in on me from all sides—first seven or eight, then more and more. They tumbled over each other, so that only their black muzzles were visible. I alternated between murmuring softly to them and shouting. Not one was smaller than a German shepherd. Whenever a dog came too near, I struck at it. By now the whole pack was snarling, howling, and barking so loudly that in desperation I also started yelling.

The villagers had to wake up now, I thought. But no one came.

I slowly crept back down the same path I had come, my back against the stone, looking left and right. The dogs followed me till I staggered out into an open meadow at the edge of the village. There the dogs' fury suddenly dissipated, and they trotted back to the huts, snarling, whining, snapping at each other.

Where was I to go now? I didn't want to head back down into the valley. The scare this pack of half-starved dogs had given me paled in comparison to the horror of my earlier nocturnal encounter. That creature, whose lair was somewhere in these valleys, was ten times more powerful and massive than any dog. I could not make my way over the mountains in the dark, and I was also too exhausted to continue climbing. I had no choice but to slink quietly back to the huts—whose inhabitants had probably taken their yak herds up into the mountain pastures. Tchagu, the dog-ridden hole, was my only hope.

I followed the cattle path back between the stone barrier and the woodpiles to the dwellings. I passed the holding pens without attracting the dogs, entered one of the courtyards through a low opening between piles of firewood, and walked toward the house: The door was padlocked. I decided to climb up the ladder to the open loft. Crouching between the floorboards and the shingles, I groped my way to a stone fireplace. Hunched over my backpack, I listened to the stillness of the night. Looking over my shoulder one last time, I stripped down to my underwear and crawled into my sleeping bag. A few minutes later, before my heartbeat and my breathing had even slowed, I fell asleep.

I sat up, torn from a deep, dreamless sleep. I thought I had heard voices. Bewildered, I peered out of the loft's triangular-shaped opening onto a ridge under the starry Himalayan sky. I had not been mistaken. I could hear steps, murmuring, and hissing. Someone was barking orders. A shower of stones came pelting onto the floorboards next to me.

Startled and still half in my sleeping bag, I crawled behind the fireplace for cover. Now there were more voices below and they grew louder. I couldn't stay hidden up in the loft. I had to come down before they dragged me out and beat me to death.

I crouched by the loft opening, almost naked, clutching my sleeping bag and clothes under my right arm, holding my backpack in my left. I hesitated for a few seconds in the moonlight at the top of the stepladder, but when I saw the grimy faces of men swinging cudgels and torches, I immediately climbed down from the loft into the courtyard. They grabbed my belongings before my feet even touched the ground, and one of the men held up a lantern to my face. I stood before them—thin, bleary-eyed, making submissive gestures—confronted by their anger, their cudgels, and their curiosity. I must have looked pitiful. The horde of wild and ragged men first started murmuring, then broke out into laughter. They weren't glaring at me anymore. Some of them whispered among themselves, others shouted questions at me I didn't understand. They began slipping swords and knives back into the leather or silver sheaths that hung from their belts.

I started stammering to them about my encounter with the yeti. I knew just about enough Tibetan to ask for some buttermilk and a place to sleep, so to describe what I had seen I used gestures and fragments of pidgin English, Nepalese, Urdu, and Tibetan. Miraculously, they understood my tale and knew right away what I was talking about.

Frantically, I told them all I could. The beast had walked on two legs, looked much stronger than a man, and was as tall as the stepladder up to the loft. It whistled by blowing air between its tongue and its upper jaw (I tried to imitate this for their benefit). And the stench! (I pinched my nose.) Even its tracks smelled like a mix of frozen garlic, rancid fat, and dung.

Two tall, gaunt Tibetans, their faces half-hidden beneath wide, broad-brimmed hats, motioned for me to follow them into their house. I had managed by then to put on my pants and my shirt. Grabbing my sleeping bag, I followed them between the walls and the woodpiles into a courtyard full of baskets and horse manure. Bending down, I entered the hut through a narrow door. One of the men pointed with his wooden club to the sleeping area near the fireplace while the other man bolted the door from the inside. I rolled out my mat and my sleeping bag. The first man put some wood in the fireplace and knelt on the floor to blow on the embers. Dull sparks and smoke billowed up, and then the fire started. In the pleasant glow of the flames the scattered objects in the room no longer looked like a confused jumble. Yak-hair ropes hung from the walls next to leather straps and an ornamental saddle. Piles of furs, stuffed sacks, and a few wooden racks lay on the floor. These racks were hauling saddles for the yaks. Two pots stood in the corner—a large one of hammered copper for water, and an aluminum one for buttermilk.

I was too tired to feel hunger, but my tongue and throat were parched from days of breathing through my mouth and from the fear of the past few hours. I begged them for some buttermilk.

One of the men put a wooden bowl in front of me filled with a grayish mush containing particles of soot. I downed it without bothering to spit out the soot. The other man was slowly and reverently pounding butter tea in a knee-high cylinder, all the while glancing over at me. They wanted to know how I had come here from Dege and why the Chinese hadn't locked me up. I laughed and showed them a document, a sort of permit, which had been issued in Lhasa, but which they couldn't read.

"There was a storm in Dege, with thunder and lightning," I tried telling them in my broken Tibetan. "I sheltered with a Tibetan family in a hut by the roadside. At midnight the floodwaters came. Loudspeakers shouted orders. People were screaming. But only a couple of houses below the road from Chengdu to Lhasa were flooded. And as the cleanup began, I escaped the Chinese."

"Escaped?"

"Before dawn. The Chinese had already locked me up once for a whole week."

One of the men shook the steaming butter tea into the wooden bowl I had eaten from. I continued with my tale.

"The road to Qamdo was cut off, so I had to walk. I spent the night in roadside inns or in the tents of yak nomads. Twice in stables. I walked for days in the rain. I hid during the day and walked through the night. The forests everywhere have been cut down and the old caravan roads were either washed away or so muddy that I often slipped and fell."

I pointed with some pride at my dirty trousers. My hosts laughed.

"Most of the time I ate *tukpa* [soup]. I drank *sho* [yogurt] and water from the springs. The day before yesterday I crossed the Shaka-La River with a yak caravan. The drivers threw my backpack onto a yak's back between two sacks, and I followed behind. After traveling down a steep slope we stopped to rest, and they offered me *tara* [buttermilk], *tsha* [tea], and *tsampa* [barley flour]. Then we went our separate ways, and I got as far as the Tokatchu monastery."

"*Tsampa?*" one of them offered. I shook my head. I wanted to sleep. The two looked at me expectantly and continued throwing twigs into the fire. They wanted to know how I had managed to escape the monster.

"Right after I left Alado, I found the path again. The creature came out of the underbrush. His head was almost as big as a yak's, but without the horns, and with dark fur. He rose on his hind legs, turned, and disappeared. His back was red."

"*Chemo?*" both men asked with one voice, uttering this word with such fear in their voices that my encounter now suddenly seemed even more terrifying. But their fear was also tinged with respect. They were obviously surprised that I had managed to survive my long trek through the darkness. "Chemo!" one of the men whispered, and shaking his head, he poured me some more butter tea. He wasn't wearing shoes.

"Chemo," I repeated. "Is that a bear?"

No, no, my hosts gestured. They told me *tom* is the word for bear, and that the tom live farther down the mountain, in the forests. Tom have shorter legs, a white patch shaped like a half-moon on their chest, and are otherwise black. They are dangerous, said my hosts, but they're not chemos. The way they said *chemo* again indicated to me both fear and veneration. Was this, I wondered sleepily, the phantom we in the West call the abominable snowman?

I must have dozed off in the middle of the conversation. In my sleep I could hear the crackling of the firewood in the fireplace, then the voices died down and the world fell silent.

The sun was streaming through the window openings when I woke, and the air smelled of stale smoke and melted fat. The hut was empty. I opened the door and stepped out of the twilight of the Tibetan hut into the midsummer sunlight. When my eyes grew accustomed to the light, I saw that I was standing in a high valley. The slopes of the steep mountains above it were gray.

My hosts emerged from another hut, followed in single file by the other villagers. They gave me yogurt, barley flour, and buttermilk for breakfast. By ten o'clock my backpack was ready and a one-eyed man offered to carry it for me. I followed him into the valley, then we made our way westward and up the slopes. We trekked past rocky streams and mountain villages, along a trail that often disappeared, moving deeper into the highlands. The mountain ridges grew higher and steeper, and behind them were even higher ridges, followed by more valleys and plateaus.

At the edge of one desolate mountain pasture were signs of an encampment and sheep grazing. My taciturn guide pointed at the ground between two knee-high rocks.

"Chemo!" he said brusquely.

I saw immense footprints. I bent down and realized that these rocks, weighing a couple of hundred pounds each, had been moved or rolled about that very night.

"Chemo?" I asked somewhat uncertainly, looking up at my guide. What was I to think?

He nodded and pointed at the rocks. *"Chemo,"* he repeated. "They lift big rocks, looking for food. And they throw rocks, like this!" He let his right arm hang down and then quickly flicked his hand backward. "They also kill goats, sheep, and even yaks."

"They live so high up in the mountains?"

"Usually they live in the forests. But in the summer they follow the nomads to the highest mountain meadows. They climb up to the snow line, just like yaks. They cross glaciers to get from one high valley to the next. They carry their children on their backs when they cross rivers or steep ravines."

"Chemos have children?"

"We call them children."

I stood in front of the large stones and looked beyond the slopes at the rock face that towered up into the deep blue of the sky. What would such a massive creature feed on at this altitude?

"This chemo of yours *must* be a bear!" I said after a while.

"He is like a bear but also like a man. He eats what we eat: barley, meat, fruit, berries, vegetables, roots, nettles. And he lives where we live. He blinks his eyes when the sunlight is bright. He looks like"— he hesitated for a moment—"a bear or an enormous monkey."

Behind the next mountain ridge was Tatu, the final high-pasture settlement and the place I hoped to spend the night. Before my good-natured guide and backpack carrier departed, I asked him to draw a chemo for me. We sat on a rock, and he drew a sketch of an animal I did not recognize.

He took the money I gave him, slipping it into a small crescent-shaped leather bag that hung like a dagger from his belt. Laughing, he stuck his tongue out at me as a friendly farewell gesture, turned toward the valley, and left.

Climbing higher and higher into the rugged terrain, I was increasingly forced to make tiring detours, because streams and gullies had washed the trail away. Soon all I could see of my former guide was a dark spot moving over the gray of the boulder-strewn slopes, and then farther down among the ocher-brown of the furrows. A vulture circled high above him.

I rested and studied the terrain with my binoculars. There were no signs of my animals. I reflected upon what I had learned about this creature called the *chemo*. It was nocturnal, larger than a man, and yet not a bear. But nor could it belong to any anthropoid species. The *Gigantopithecus,* an early hominid of enormous size, had been extinct for millennia. Cave bears had disappeared from Southeast Asia over ten thousand years ago. Both had lived in mountain and forest habitats and once dwelt in the Himalayas, as archaeologists had proved.

When I arrived in the village of Tatu, a group of children invited me into a nomad tent and I was allowed to sleep among them on furs on the ground. The following day before sunrise I climbed to a pass at an altitude of over sixteen thousand feet, beyond which lay a seemingly endless plateau. Farther to the north were chains of low-lying mountains. And beyond them were the frozen deserts of northern Tibet.

I turned around again and looked across the steppes and the cirques covered with edelweiss, down into the valleys up which I had climbed. The distant clumps of bushes looked like tufts of down on the mountainsides. Farther down lay the black ravines with their dense conifer forests.

My brushes with the chemo—if that's what it was—had changed everything. I had gone off in search of one legend and been captured by a completely different one—that of the yeti, tales of which the Sherpas had brought with them to Nepal during their long march out of their Tibetan homelands. Finding the yeti would mean locating the source of its legend. Had the yeti legend originated during the Sherpas' trek from Kham to Solo Khumbu, a legacy of their origins? Or was it shared by all Tibetans living in the snow country? Century after century came stories of a creature that would suddenly appear and then disappear, a creature that with time had taken on increasingly human characteristics. Whether these stories were fantasy, nightmare, or true was unimportant. Legends have moved whole nations and kept them together, and it was legend that fired my curiosity—even though the creature I had confronted was more than just a legend.

The mountains that I knew so well now seemed shrouded in mystery. Though I had climbed them many times, they had a wildness I had not fully appreciated until now. Had Sabine, my girlfriend, not been waiting for me in Lhasa, I would have plunged back into this strange new world.

I looked back one last time at the mountain ranges and valleys I had crossed. What had I seen? A yeti? A chemo? Were they the same creature?

2

REUNITED IN LHASA

In Lharigo I was chased away from a nomad encampment—children threw stones at me, dogs attacked me, and women waved pots of flour at me as if exorcising an evil spirit. I didn't dare talk to anyone about the yeti.

Toward midnight I found a house with lights on and walked toward it, calling out. I entered the forecourt, surprised that nobody tried to chase me away and that there were no dogs. I should have taken it as a warning: Tibetans keep dogs, the Chinese eat them. The door was ajar and I poked my head in, ready to run at a moment's notice.

I could see a dim light. A man's voice asked me to come upstairs. I made my way through the low-ceilinged basement and climbed some stairs to the first floor.

I realized too late that I had stumbled into a police station. Yet, to my surprise and relief, rather than arresting me, the official on duty gave me a bottle of beer and told me I could spend the night in an empty cell. It had been ages since I had slept in a bed. Weeks since I'd had a beer. My host, a well-groomed Chinese soldier, wanted to know what I was doing in these parts. I stared into my beer glass and muttered:

"I came from Lhasa and want to get back to Lhasa."

This seemed to satisfy him. He brought me a bowl of cooked rice and then went off to bed. He didn't bolt the door to my cell, but I was too tired to think of escape, and too grateful to finally be able to sleep through an entire night.

The scurrying feet of mice across the wood floor woke me with a start. It was morning. I looked around in the dim light. The room contained no furniture besides an iron bed. A newspaper was plastered to the rough mortar of a wall. Next to it was a picture of a young-looking Mao. I looked out the cell's tiny window at the milk-white mountain ridges over which I had crossed.

A few days later, I came upon a paved road somewhere between Nachu and Lhasa. Behind me lay the pastel-colored folds of the Amdo highlands, and before me was a mountain range shimmering blue on the horizon, a frozen tidal wave. Its glacial peaks, towering into puffy cotton-wool clouds, looked like wave crests.

Exhausted and sick of being alone, I trekked parallel to the road leading south, carefully maintaining a distance of about a hundred yards. Long convoys of field-green military vehicles kept rolling past me, disappearing into a hollow far off in the distance. It was clear that Tibet was being governed by the Chinese army.

Another convoy passed, then another. A distant spot would grow into a train of vehicles that would rumble past, then diminish into the size of a toy train and disappear. Often a full hour would elapse between the time the first truck appeared and the last one moved out of sight.

It was difficult traveling to Lhasa unnoticed by the Chinese.

Only Tibetans would give me a lift to the capital without asking questions, but they went either on foot on back roads or waited in the villages for buses that were monitored by the Chinese—and therefore not an option.

The vehicles that passed me—trucks carrying road workers, jeeps, buses, and military convoys—were Chinese. The road from Golmud to Lhasa seemed to belong to them alone.

Then I spotted a brightly colored and dilapidated truck that had pulled over to the side of the road. I moved nearer. There was no other traffic, so I climbed up the embankment. A group of Tibetans were about to climb back into the truck. I hailed them. They were on their way to Lhasa, they told me. I could ride with them for a handful of Rimbimbi notes.

A few moments later I was lying on an iron platform the size of a bed above the driver's cab, hidden beneath a tarpaulin and packed between furs, spare auto parts, and a couple of tough-looking men from Amdo. The smell of mold, motor oil, and sweat was nearly overpowering.

I felt reasonably safe. It would have been hard to recognize me as European amid all the bodies, baskets, and tarpaulins, among hats, capes, and colored ribbons. My hair was tousled by the wind and my nose as sunburned as those of my fellow travelers. I was sure I could blend in so long as we kept moving. I had shaved off my beard before setting out for east Tibet, and during my journey I'd used the scissors in my pocketknife to trim my beard. I had not wanted to turn up in remote villages looking like a wild man. Now my beard was so dusty that it looked gray, barely distinguishable from the rest of my face.

Almost a week had passed since my encounter with the creature, and I still didn't have answers to all the questions whirling around in my head. I wondered if the men next to me knew more than I did, but I didn't know how to start a conversation with them. What should I call the monster whose image in my mind had become indistinct?

In the recent past, Europeans trying to get to Lhasa had been turned away. At the turn of the century, the legendary Swedish explorer Sven Hedin reported that two travelers trying to reach the Forbidden City had been tortured and killed. A handful of Englishmen had lived there, and later the German zoologist Ernst Schäfer. But traveling through the Lhasa valley was not dangerous for me. I had a valid visa and was no longer traveling though prohibited territories.

Finally, among the clouds of dust gathering in the warm afternoon sun, Lhasa appeared in front of us. The truck made its way fitfully through the traffic, honking and groaning past long rows of low houses. Behind us were high ridges, a landscape without a horizon.

The suburbs of Lhasa seemed like one big construction site. Chinese were everywhere, overseeing Tibetan laborers, or working noisy machinery that spat out pungent clouds of smoke. Historical buildings had been torn down and replaced by concrete barracks with corrugated-iron roofs. Only the Potala Palace and a few temples were spared, as museums for us tourists.

We drove along the former Linkor, the pilgrim gallery at the foot of Potala, now lined with concrete blocks, Chinese banners, bicycles, tractors, and goats. Lhasa had become a city like thousands of others in Asia—its medieval feel was gone. Beijing officials were now the rulers, and Lhasa, rather than being the "holy city," was merely the capital of the Autonomous Province of Tibet. Tibetan art had been supplanted by Chinese kitsch, horses by bicycles, and lamas by soldiers. Only the gilded pagodas of the Potala still glittered high above the noise and confusion of everyday life. But even the Potala, once the residence and headquarters of the Dalai Lama, now seemed sterile. Somewhere nearby, on one of the new main streets, lay Sabine's and my hotel, the Tibet Guest House.

I pounded my fist on the roof of the driver's cab. The truck pulled up near the crooked walls of a row of huts, and I jumped off.

I thanked them—*Tu jey chey!*—and looked around. This part of the old town would also soon disappear, I thought as I heaved my backpack onto my shoulders. I waved at the driver and walked off. The truck, bearing the logo LIBERATION, rattled off in the opposite direction.

An hour earlier I had been staring up at Lhasa through the uncannily low-lying blue skies of Tibet and had seen bright prayer flags fluttering from gabled rooftops and trees. Now I stood in the shadow of high-rise buildings and the din of chaotic traffic, surrounded by concrete and smog. No wonder the spirit of the old Tibetans was broken, and only young exiles such as Jamyang Norbu in India continued to fight for independence. As Norbu once told me, "Regardless of what the Tibetan people have had to endure— torture, imprisonment, hunger, and the insanity of the Cultural Revolution—nothing has been as threatening to the survival of the Tibetan people as the relatively peaceful migration of the Chinese into Tibet."

Anyone walking through Lhasa can see that the Tibetans are being pushed out. Highlanders from the northern and eastern steppes who visit this holy city are confused by how foreign the city seems.

I arrived at the Tibetan Guest House and asked for Sabine Stehle. The Tibetan girl at the reception desk said no one of that name was staying there. She sounded so sure that I immediately turned around and walked outside, to hide my disappointment. Maybe Sabine had checked into a different hotel, I thought.

I set out on foot for the Lhasa Hotel, the only place in town that resembled a Western hotel. She wasn't there either.

I made my way back to the old town. Had she left because I had stayed away so long? I wondered anxiously. I couldn't believe she would do such a thing without leaving me a message. She had all our money for the trip home. What if she hadn't made it to Lhasa? That seemed unlikely unless the roads had been blocked, or the plane from Chengdu to Lhasa fully booked. Had she had an accident? Had the Chinese police arrested her? I returned to the Tibet

Guest House, scenarios spinning through my head, and approached the receptionist.

"There is no Miss Stehle is registered here," she told me with the same air of conviction.

"Could she have been staying here two, three weeks ago?" I asked, trying hard not to sound desperate.

We looked through the register and found her name. She had shared a room with an Austrian woman whose name I didn't recognize. The two of them had left the hotel together.

"Where is Miss Stehle now?"

"I have no idea."

"She must have left a message for me!"

"There is no message. I'm sorry."

I went back out into the street and walked to Parkor, the shopping area in the center of town, and to an old house that belonged to some relatives of Tarchen, an exiled Tibetan freedom fighter who had been our interpreter before he had gone into hiding in Kanze in east Tibet. He had left before the Chinese police could arrest and imprison him.

Tarchen wasn't there. His relatives hadn't heard from him since he had accompanied Sabine and me to the holy lake of Koko Nor in early June. Our car had crashed, but the three of us, unharmed, had managed to evade police roadblocks. We had been detained by military patrols but managed to escape and had finally made it to Kanze. I told Tarchen's anxious aunts and uncles the whole story. "Tarchen is clever. They won't catch him," I said to comfort them, then left.

Unable to think of anything else to do, I went back to the Tibet Guest House for a third time. The girl at the desk smiled at me sympathetically.

She greeted me with "I really am sorry, but I can't help you."

I asked her if I could take a quick look at the room Sabine had stayed in, underlining my request with plaintive gestures. She told me the room was vacant, then handed me the key and pointed upstairs.

I climbed a wooden staircase to the second floor and started down a corridor. I saw the silhouette of a woman stepping out from one of the rooms into the bright sunlight streaming in from one of the square windows. Without looking toward me, she turned and locked her door. Her hand movements gave her away—it was Sabine.

I took a few steps toward her. She, too, seemed to recognize me. I had never seen her looking so frail and distracted.

Seeing Sabine again was more of a shock than a relief. I stood, silent and apprehensive. She also just stood there, staring at me. I couldn't think straight. After all the excitement, the anticipation, the hope and fear, the dread of not finding her, I was too bewildered to embrace her. I was still so obsessed by the thought that she might have left forever that I was incapable of even asking how she was.

"I saw a yeti," I blurted out suddenly, breaking the silence. Sabine looked at me with astonishment. Then, as if we suddenly realized the absurdity of it all, we fell into each other's arms.

Sabine explained what had happened. She had been ill with dysentery and hadn't left her room for a week. Nobody in the hotel had noticed. As far as the hotel was concerned, the room had been vacant since her Austrian roommate, a casual acquaintance, had checked out, and no one seemed to have missed the second key.

I put my backpack on the floor of her tiny room. Sabine watched me, silent. From embarrassment and guilt, as well as my uneasiness at her silence, I started blathering about the yeti.

"They say the yeti lives in caves and sleeps during the day. He only goes out at night. The tracks he leaves show that he always walks on two legs. He doesn't only growl, he whistles and throws stones, too."

Sabine didn't even look up. I pressed on.

"You know what? The natives told me that yetis—they call them *chemos*—have fur that can be red, black, or gray. Some of them also have white heads. In rare cases they can be completely white, or flecked, like yaks."

Sabine sat hunched forward on the edge of the bed, her head propped on her hands. Finally she broke her silence.

"Yeah, right, and these yeti women with their enormous breasts grab human males and drag them into their caves!"

"That is exactly what the Khampa say about the chemo," I noted seriously.

"I think you've been on the road too long, Reinhold. What you saw was a bear."

"You mean a Tibetan bear?"

"Or a panda."

"What I saw wasn't a panda. And it wasn't a Himalayan bear either. It was something else. It doesn't sleep on the snow in winter, it sleeps in caves. There are sometimes ferocious battles among rivals over caves," I added, suddenly remembering that someone had told me that.

"You're sure it couldn't have been a brown bear?" asked Sabine.

"Have you ever seen a brown bear with white fur on its head?"

"And did you see this white-headed yeti?"

"No, but do you remember the sky burial north of Lhasa?" I asked.

"Yes."

"Would you have believed before the sun rose that nothing, absolutely nothing, would remain of the dead man's body?"

"No."

"Well, a yeti is as difficult to imagine as a sky burial, if you weren't there yourself."

Sabine lay on the bed, listening. Then she started telling me about her own adventure. She described her journey, much of which had taken place in horrendous downpours. She had seen the wreckage of a truck that had crashed, killing two Americans. She spoke of a seven-foot-tall Khampa, a native of Kham, whom she had hired to help her escape from the Tarchen monastery to Chengdu. The more she recounted, the more alive she became. I felt as if I had her back.

Sabine brought up the subject of the yeti a few days later: "Where will these animals go when the Chinese cut down the last forests?"

"They live well above the tree line."

"And the Himalayan black bears?"

"They'll move somewhere else. The Tibetans in Kham call them *tom,* and they live farther down, in the forests. Tom have no real mythological significance, maybe because they can be found from Pakistan to northern India and the Himalayas, all the way down to southern China, Vietnam, Korea, and Japan."

"Tell me again why are you so sure that the animal you saw wasn't a bear."

"Partly because of the way Tibetans talk about him and fear him. They say he can kill with a single punch."

"A bear can break a goat's spine with a single swipe of its paw."

"Bears attack their prey by tumbling down the mountainside. These creatures stand upright when they attack. And their fur is much longer—so long that supposedly it falls into their eyes."

"It's amazing how you shape everything to fit your theories, Reinhold."

"One encounter can change you. Everything changes—the whole landscape. In the mountains and upper valleys of Nepal, and in Solo Khumbu, yetis are no longer a presence. In Nepal the yeti is only a specter. But in eastern Tibet it is a reality."

Sabine smiled. "If you really want to see a monster, just take a look at yourself in the mirror."

We both burst out laughing.

The following day, looking down from the Potala, we could see that Lhasa was a city divided in two. Half was characterized by the old Tibetan architectural style with its square brick houses and flat roofs, the other half by corrugated-iron roofs, barracks, and factories.

In the afternoon we walked through the old town, where the bazaar has come back to life. Bartering has boomed along the unpaved, winding back streets. Tiny stores offer tourists everything from prayer flags to gold-plated bronzes. I saw Chinese informants keeping an eye on the market. The piercing stench of rancid fat, incense, and urine hung in the air.

Tibetans are passionate traders, and the decades-long ban on private trade had hit them almost as hard as the ban on religious practices. But now that the ban has been partially lifted, what are they supposed to trade with? Most consumer goods are available in the Chinese-run supermarkets, and few are interested in the wool, butter, and jewelry the Tibetans have to offer. And yet nomads sell their handicrafts in the bazaar or barter sheep for *tsampa*. In the middle of one back street we saw a dentist, surrounded by a crowd, plying his trade.

In Parkor, the prayer street surrounding the Jokhang temple, we saw faces from every corner of the Tibetan highlands: Khampas from eastern Tibet, natives of Amdo, and a few yak nomads from the Chang Tang Desert. Grinning, I kept shouting "Chemo!" into the stores of the bazaar with a mixture of expectation and high spirits. I hoped to find at least a few bones, or a pelt—proof that chemos were yetis, that a living creature and a creature of legend could be one and the same.

How these night creatures had managed to survive was deeply mysterious. But how they could die without leaving a trace was a deeper one. The Neanderthals died out many millennia ago, and yet we have found their remains. If yetis or chemos really did exist, there had to be bones, or at least a hide.

But in the markets of Lhasa no one would even talk to me about them, and I wondered why. Was it superstition? Was this mysterious creature perceived as unclean? In Lhasa the three professions of lowest rank are metallurgy, animal slaughtering, and undertaker. Quick and efficient disposing of corpses has always been a problem in Tibet. As cremation is expensive, dead bodies are often left outside for the birds, and corpses are burned or buried only when birds won't eat them. The bodies of small children and the very poor might be thrown into rivers to avoid funeral costs. Morticians or makers of funeral paraphernalia tend to be shy and live in seclusion. Was the same true of people who had seen a chemo?

The yeti haunted my dreams. During the night, between deep sleep and nightmare, I found myself climbing once more through the forested ravines of eastern Tibet.

L hasa was depressing. Throughout the city Sabine and I found apathy, drunkenness, hopelessness. Cheap alcohol—Chinese beer, rice wine—was being sold everywhere. Beijing is happy to subsidize what destroys the Tibetans.

When Tibet was still a monastic state, the people had suffered under the yoke of the lamas, the priestly caste. Now they are suffering under communism. Shell horns used to summon the monks, who would gather around their silver teapots and their chalices filled with *tsampa*. Now Chinese officials bark out orders over loudspeakers. Free and independent thought has long been suppressed in Tibet—and that suppression culminated with the invasion of the Chinese and their relentless assimilationist politics. The people of Tibet suffer terribly under Chinese rule; resistance brings torture and death.

Feeling depressed, we left for Katmandu. On the road to Shigatse we encountered hordes of pilgrims heading toward the holy shrines in the western regions of the country, murmuring mantras, offering alms, and carrying prayer wheels. On the outskirts of the Shigatse the pilgrims circled the Tashi Lhumpo monastery, walking in single file around its walls, while military convoys rumbled through the new part of town with its corrugated-iron roofs. Night had fallen by the time we had settled in at our hostel. Above us, in the dim moonlight, towered the monastery, which had miraculously managed to escape destruction by the Chinese invaders. Tashi Lhumpo is one of the most beautiful monasteries in Tibet. Now a museum, its golden rooftops and myriad intertwined buildings of red and white cubes are among the finest examples of Tibetan architecture in existence. Here once lived lamas, obedient slaves to centuries-old dogmas they were forbidden to question.

When we left Shigatse the next morning, smoke from sacrificial fires lit before the *gompa*—the monastery—was billowing into the skies. The breeze smelled of juniper trees and tasted of dust. Prayer flags flapped, reminding me of the old Tibet. If symbols could only change reality, I thought sadly.

For four months each year the Tibetans plow, sow, and harvest their fields, as they have done since time immemorial. Neither machinery nor collective farming has had much effect on this cycle in the mountain villages. In the past, a large part of the harvest went to the monasteries; today Chinese trucks haul it off.

We drove in a jeep between barley fields toward Tingri, down the dusty road that connects Lhasa with Sinkiang. Our first stop was Shegar, a small town at the foot of a mountain atop which sat a monastery called Shegar Dzong. The monastery had fallen victim to the Cultural Revolution. Built a thousand feet in the air—so high that on a clear day from the battlements you could see Chomolungma, Mount Everest, which the Himalayans once worshiped as a god—the monastery was in ruins. Below us, the schoolchildren of the village practiced marching beneath a red flag.

Wherever there were roads in Tibet, the Red Guards had systematically and mercilessly laid waste to the old Tibet. Only the highlands, accessible solely by footpaths, had escaped devastation. There some ancient ways have managed to survive. As did the legend of the yeti.

Aside from destroying their traditions, what has communism and the Cultural Revolution given those Tibetans who had managed to survive? There are schools and first-aid stations, even in small villages, but the standard of living has risen only slightly. Everyone has to work. In Tibet, child labor seems as inevitable as sandstorms, cold, and heat.

Sabine and I had grown accustomed to *tsampa* and salty tea with yak butter. We had a harder time stomaching the imperious tone of our Chinese driver and our interpreter, who were escorting us to the Nepalese border.

Before 1950, there were five thousand monasteries or *tshorten*—shrines built on roadsides—in Tibet, and every fifth Tibetan was a monk. The lamas disappeared with the arrival of the Red Guards, and many of the holy sites were ransacked. Only a few dozen monasteries were spared. Of the one hundred thousand lamas living in Tibet in 1950, perhaps one thousand remain today. The Chinese could only destroy the symbols of Lamaism, however, not the landscape, which lies at the root of the religion.

Before the invasion, houses were freshly whitewashed for the New Year festivities. The new rulers banned such gratuitous embellishments, just as they disallowed the wearing of the bright traditional costumes—a law that proved unenforceable because everyone continued wearing them. The monastic nation had turned into a Chinese province, and Chinese roadside villages sprang up next to Tibetan settlements. They quickly crumbled again, the huts made of brick and corrugated iron undone by heat and frost.

In Tingri we made a short stop to visit some nomads. The yak-hair tents smelled of animals and rancid butter. Yak dung, the nomads' most important source of fuel, lay piled up in heaps in front of the tents.

A man named Gyaltsen Norbu came out to greet us. I asked him what the Tibetan name was for the animal that Sherpas and tourists called yeti. "Chemo," he replied. He took us to a monastery at the edge of the great Tingri plain where relics of a yeti had once been preserved. He told us that traders had brought them over Nangpa La to Khumbu.

It had been the Sherpas of Khumbu, the farmers living on the

other side of the Himalayas, who had first told me of the yeti during my expeditions to Lhotse, Mount Everest, Cho Oyu, and to
the holy mountain of Ama Dablam. Every Sherpa seemed to have
had tales to tell about the yeti, and once a year they celebrate
Mani Rimbu, which roughly means "all will be well," a feast during which they worship their nature gods, and a masked figure—
a yeti—appears. They and the exiled Tibetans of Katmandu, I
thought, would help me solve its mystery.

3

CONFUSION IN KATMANDU

The quest for the yeti goes back as far as Alexander the Great, who in 326 B.C. set out with his army of Greeks to conquer the Indus Valley. Alexander pushed almost all the way to Kashmir. The yeti, people said, could not breathe at low altitudes, and this is why the conquering Alexander was not presented with one.

Pliny the Elder, who in 79 A.D. fell victim to his own thirst for knowledge in the eruption of Mount Vesuvius, describes a yeti-like creature in his *Natural History:* "In the Land of the Satyrs, in the mountains that lie to the east of India, live creatures that are extremely swift, as they can run both on four feet and on two. They have human-like bodies, and because of their swiftness can only be caught when they are ill or old."

Aelianus, who lived 150 years later and was Emperor Septimus' head priest, wrote in *Animal Stories* "of an animal reminiscent of Satyrs that lives in the Indian mountains":

> If one enters the mountains neighboring India one comes upon lush, overgrown valleys. The Indians call this region Koruda. Animals that look like Satyrs roam these valleys. They are covered with shaggy hair and have a long horse's tail. When left to themselves, they stay in the forest and eat tree sprouts. But when they hear the din of approaching hunters and the barking of dogs, they run with incredible speed to hide in mountain caves. For they are masters at mountain climbing. They also repel approaching humans by hurling stones down at them.

These Satyrs Aelianus describes have qualities still attributed to the yeti today, and which are also true of the chemo, the animal I was beginning to believe was closely associated with the yeti and its legend.

In the twenty-sixth song of Milarepa, a yogi poet and hermit who lived in the Himalayas almost a millennium ago, a creature similar to the yeti makes an appearance. The poet's description matches that of a creature in a two-hundred-year-old medicine book found by the anthropologist Emmanuel Vleck.

Scientists have sometimes attempted to draw conclusions about the yeti from two-million-year-old bones found in the vicinity of the Himalayan range. The British zoologists John Napier and Charles Stonor proved that orangutans could have survived on the Asian continent into the eighteenth and nineteenth centuries. By 1976, however, their habitat had become limited to the Indonesian islands of Sumatra and Borneo. *Orang utan* means "forest man" in Malay, and its fossils have been found in northern India, Pakistan, the Chinese province of Yunnan, and in the western foothills of the Himalayas.

Katmandu, the capital of Nepal, is not the ideal place to begin researching the yeti. The mountains to the north of the city are covered year-round in snow and much too far away. They are a backdrop, nothing more. Yet nowhere in the world are there as many reports of the yeti as in Katmandu. The stories that Sherpas and other porters tell after returning from treks into the glacier regions constantly increase in number. It is impossible to tell which are based on real sightings and which are fantasies or retellings of older tales.

On the streets of Katmandu the yeti is both a legend and a highly salable commodity. Images of it appear on everything from T-shirts and ice cream to package tours—even airline stocks. Nobody wants the legend linked to reality, except perhaps for a handful of scientists and explorers—but they are not taken seriously. After a century of research the only thing the scientists have managed to prove conclusively is the embarrassing fact that all the yeti relics kept in various lama monasteries are fakes.

The idea of the yeti being some kind of monster spread from the Sherpa territories and kindled the imaginations of people throughout the world. Sherpa guides told the climbers they escorted stories about a creature that was, they said, halfway between a man and a beast. When famous climbers such as Frank Smythe, H. William Tilman, and John Hunt reported having seen the footprints of a gigantic creature that might correspond to the yeti of the Sherpa legends, scientists and journalists banded together to set up expeditions.

The first Western description of a "hairy wild man" roaming the mountains of Asia came from Mongolia, written by a fifteenth-century European mercenary. Today, most people living in remote Himalayan regions describe the yeti as an apelike bear that lives below the snow line. He is worshiped in the Hindu Kush as a supernatural being. For many Sikkimese, this "wild man" is a forest deity that only appears to the righteous. Sacrifices are made to him before hunting expeditions.

The tales from Sikkim and Tibet continue to arouse people's interest, particularly in Nepal, where tourism has grown to become the main source of income. The yeti is a hot topic as much among the poor in the streets as among the rich in their salons. An English journalist in the 1920s heated things up by rendering the yeti's Tibetan name, *migyu*, as "abominable snowman"—a mistranslation, by the way. The label has stuck to this day.

How the yeti legend grew to the proportions it has is no longer ascertainable. Had there always been stories of a strange beast roaming the forests and ice deserts of Tibet, frightening off human intruders and killing yaks? All the time, of course, I was wondering about what I had seen on the way to Lhasa and Tingri. I thought I might find an answer in Katmandu, where everyone seemed to know about the yeti.

Tamel, the tourist quarter of Katmandu, proved such fun that I didn't give the yeti any further thought. The old bazaar was loud and overcrowded, but I had never been anywhere more intensely alive. The back streets echoed with the ringing of countless bicycle bells, and a thick throng of people crowded past the stalls. Everywhere was an aroma of spices, incense, and rotting fruit.

A spotted white bull lolled about in the middle of the street, and like everyone else I carefully crept around it as if it were a sleeping predator. Bulls are considered holy, and no passerby would dare disturb it, let alone chase it away.

I went to the Two Snow Lions, an antiques shop, to see Gyaltsen, an old friend of mine who had fled Tibet with the Dalai Lama in 1959. *Tashi delek!* he shouted when he saw me. He called for tea to be brought, for he knew that as a passionate collector of all things Tibetan I would have a hard time resisting his treasures if I stayed long enough. This time, I said, all I wanted was information. But Gyaltsen was set on selling me two Tibetan animal carpets that he had at home. He showed me pictures of them. They seemed in mint condition. I promised I would drop by his house that evening to look at the carpets—and ask him a few questions.

Gyaltsen's wife had prepared *mo-mo*—delicious dough pockets filled with meat and vegetables—for Sabine and me. First we ate, then we got down to business. Even though they had ancient designs, I thought the carpets too expensive. I could have bought them for a third of the price in Lhasa. I interrupted the haggling by blurting out, "What do people in East Tibet call the being that the tourists here in Nepal call yeti?"

"Chemo," Gyaltsen answered quite casually, then continued his sales pitch for the carpets that lay spread out on the floor.

"It has become difficult to find Tibetan things," he told us. "The Chinese won't let anyone cross the border anymore. Just the other day two merchants got shot trying to smuggle goods out through Bhutan."

I tried concealing my interest in what Gyaltsen had said about the chemo, by carefully examining the carpets. I didn't want him to notice my excitement.

One of the carpets had a particularly mysterious look to it. Occult symbols were woven around a human figure. "Tantra," Gyaltsen said, as casually as he had said "chemo." On the other carpet were all sorts of animals, including a phoenix and snow leopards pictured among clouds and mountain peaks. The workmanship really was superb. I suddenly decided I had to have the carpets. Having just confirmed to me that the Nepalese yeti corresponded to the Tibetan *chemo,* my friend could have sold me anything.

The woolly mountaintops depicted in one of the carpets reminded me of my journey through Tibet—a trek that I didn't want anyone in Katmandu to find out about, for fear of attracting too much attention. I asked Gyaltsen if one could still find statues, wall carpets, or antique jewelry with chemo motifs in Lhasa.

"No, in Tibet you can't find anything with the chemo on it," he said. "It's only here in Katmandu that the chemo is depicted. Here it is displayed everywhere, for all kinds of reasons."

"And can one buy Tibet-related ware in Katmandu?"

"Yes, but everything is much cheaper in Tibet. The problem is getting it over the border."

I shrugged my shoulders and grinned.

Gyaltsen grinned back at me. "You are a climber. The Chinese haven't posted any guards high up in the mountains."

I laughed, imagining myself climbing across the Himalayas with a backpack full of smuggled booty. For my next trip to Tibet I was planning to obtain a permit from Beijing, and all I intended to smuggle out of the country were a few facts.

"Do you think the Chinese will let you into Tibet?" Gyaltsen asked me.

"I don't see why not. It's just a question of which regions one wants to travel in."

"You must go and see my family in Lhasa. They'll help you."

"In my search for the yeti?"

"Why not? But I don't think there are any left," he said after a few moments of silence. "Not to mention that chemos bring bad luck."

It was well past midnight by the time Sabine and I returned to our hotel, with me carrying both carpets under my arm. I was exhilarated. The visit with Gyaltsen had convinced me that the chemo was real, and that somewhere behind it lay the mystery of the yeti.

Tibetans believe that man originally emerged from the highlands surrounded by the tallest mountains on earth. To them the holy mountain Kailas is the center of the world. A thought entered my mind: Did the yeti legend figure in the myth of man's creation? Could Tibet, the home of the yeti, be the cradle of mankind?

Before setting out for Makalu, the fifth-highest mountain in the world, Sabine and I filled our days with shopping and packing. We asked everyone we met what the Tibetan word was for the creature that had come to haunt the imagination of both locals and tourists in Nepal. The answers were *chemo* and sometimes variations, such as *chemong* and *dremo*.

It was becoming clear that the chemo was real to the mountain people of Tibet, an animal imbued with human characteristics but not with human features. The yeti of the Nepalese tales, on the other hand, seemed more like a mythical creature. Still, there were traits common to the yeti and the chemo: both were nocturnal creatures, both were extremely rare, and both were frequently the subjects of tales in which they drag off a young maiden to their lair, where they then live with her and where she bears them children. I had heard such tales during my travels in Sichuan, Tibet, Nepal, and Baltistan. I had also heard the following story, or some variation of it, in Katmandu and knew it was told throughout those regions.

In the fall of 1980, in the mountains of eastern China, a group of explorers from the Chinese Academy of Sciences found the hands and feet of a "wild man" preserved in a school in the province of Zheyang. A schoolteacher had pickled them in salt, and they were in good condition. Their report caused a sensation, for it seemed to confirm that these relics belonged to an apelike man. The story behind them was incredible. One afternoon in 1957, in a remote settlement called Zhuantan, Xu Fudi, a woman in her midthirties, heard her small daughter screaming. She ran to where the child had been tending the herd and was horrified to see an apelike creature carrying her away. She instinctively grabbed a thick branch and began beating the creature until it dropped the child, who, luckily, was unharmed. A dozen or so women came running when they heard the noise and also began beating the ape-man, who was howling and crying horribly, until they finally killed him. The newspaper *Sonyang* ran a description of the beast: "The creature was covered with long brown hair, was male, and relatively young. Its teeth were white, and its eyebrows, ears, and tongue were like those of a man. Its nose was flat and its chest wide and bulging. There were undigested bamboo sprouts in its stomach."

After the explorers from the Chinese Academy of Science heard this tale, they searched the area and found dens surrounded by staves and insulated with leaves and branches, which they assumed belonged to a group of hominids.

"How does this all fit together?" I asked Ang Dorje, the Sherpa who had first told me this tale. I always dropped by Ang Dorje's house when I was in Nepal. This time I had gone to see him to find out more about the chemo. He showed me the yellowed newspaper clipping with the picture of a yeti hand, which looked like a hairy human hand. But the story sounded too incredible, and after studying the picture I felt somewhat skeptical.

"If this hand in the picture really belonged to a yeti," I said to Ang, "then what I saw wasn't a yeti."

The Sherpa looked at me and shook his head, as if giving up hope that I would ever understand.

"The only yeti is the one in your head," his son, Lakpa, suddenly said. He had been listening to our conversation with a grin on his face.

"Well, what else can I say about the yeti?" Ang Dorje asked.

"It's all a bunch of fairy tales," said his son.

"This morning I was still one of the people who believed that yetis exist," I replied. "And there are not many who do—outside of some explorers and a few Khampas. For a long time I didn't. I've been to Nepal over thirty times in the last fifteen years. I've visited monasteries and spoken with all kinds of people. I came to the conclusion that yetis existed only in legends."

"What you are saying is that the yeti is only what people imagine it to be?" asked Lakpa.

"Yes, but that's not all I'm saying. Ever since I encountered that creature in Tibet, it has become for me more than just a figment of my imagination."

I was shocked by my own words. Had I revealed too much?

"Many Tibetans say exactly the same thing," Lakpa replied.

"But the lamas from Tame and Tengpoche also talk about the yeti," I said in an attempt to steer the conversation to Solo Khumbu. "They are convinced."

"Convinced of what?"

"Convinced that there are still live yetis."

"How can a well-traveled European like you . . . ," began Lakpa.

"I have spoken to a great number of Tibetans in the past few days, also with Sherpas who have traveled all over."

"Did you hear the story about the Sherpa girl who was supposedly attacked recently by a yeti?"

"Yes."

"So what does he look like, this yeti of yours?"

"More like a bear than an ape."

"You mean some kind of bear-man?"

"Animal, not man," I replied.

"How big?"

"Maybe five to seven and a half feet tall."

"Is he dangerous?"

"Not necessarily."

"So why do people call him the abominable snowman?"

"That's just a cliché."

"*Yeti* doesn't even mean 'snowman,' " Ang Dorje added.

"I know. The yeti lives among the rocks high up in the mountains. In the snow, too. Could one translate the word *yeti* as meaning 'snow bear'?" I asked.

Father and son looked at each other. "Well, that's what it actually means," Ang Dorje said. Lakpa nodded his head.

"Snow bear, bear-man." I laughed.

"Snowman!" we all shouted.

"Nobody has taken a picture of this snowman or captured him on film, so he doesn't exist as far as I'm concerned," Lakpa said obstinately.

"Eric Shipton took a picture of a yeti footprint."

"Yes, I know those pictures. They could have been the tracks of a bear."

"That's what I'm saying. Maybe the yeti is a snow bear," I suggested.

"A bear is a bear. Yetis, if they exist, are something different."

"Preconceptions, nothing but preconceptions! What happened to your scientific curiosity?" I teased the young Sherpa.

"Sherpa Tenzing Norgay laughed at the very mention of a yeti, and he knew the Himalayas better than anyone. He never saw any. Fifty years of climbing, and not a single yeti!" Tenzing Norgay had accompanied Sir Edmund Hillary up Mount Everest in 1953; he had died only a few months earlier, in May 1986.

"But there are many others who have seen one. Basi the Greek, for instance."

Lakpa waved his hand dismissively.

"He saw a yeti in Sikkim," I insisted. "In 1925, I think."

"Unfortunately he didn't take a picture."

"Lord Hunt saw yeti footprints east of Kanchenjunga. Two prints right next to each other," Ang Dorje offered.

"But Lord Hunt says the yeti isn't a bear," Lakpa pointed out. He turned to his father. "Tenzing told me the yeti was supposed to be like a large monkey, some sort of apelike creature. Strange how it is always someone else who supposedly saw the yeti. You never meet anyone who's actually seen one himself."

"You don't believe I saw one?" I asked.

"It's very hard to believe," Ang Dorje said.

"Isn't it a little suspect that it's always one person, all alone, who runs into a yeti, who is also all alone?" Lakpa asked me.

"I'm not asking you to believe me," I replied defensively.

Lakpa laughed. "It's the same old story. A man, all alone, comes across a lone yeti."

"As if a yeti would never appear with his family in tow!" Ang Dorje joined in.

"You're right," I admitted. "Almost never have two, three, or more people seen a yeti at the same time."

I added with a grin, "Maybe this is why the yeti legends all contain an erotic element. Male yeti grabs female human playmate and drags her off to his love nest. Yeti woman takes human male as a plaything."

The two men didn't laugh.

Ang Dorje's and his son's skepticism was shared by most. So why was the yeti tale told throughout the Himalayas? A strange, shambling, manlike creature that abducted humans of the opposite sex? What about those footprints that were too large to be those of a human being and yet could not be matched with those of any known animal? What about those people living in remote villages who were in constant terror of this monster? And what about all the names it had been given over the centuries: *chemong, meti, shukpa, migo, kang-mi?*

Although the hunt for the yeti has become a popular sport in Nepal in the past fifty years, nobody has solved the mystery. As far back as 1832, Brian H. Hodson, Britain's first representative to Nepal, described an unknown creature that "moved erectly, was covered in long, dark hair, and had no tail." Back home in Britain, people dismissed his reports, along with the accounts of sightings by the local population. It wasn't until Major L. A. Waddell, a renowned Tibetan specialist, reported repeated discoveries of strange footprints in the Himalayas that Western interest was piqued, and the hunt for the hairy wild man of the land of eternal snows began in earnest.

In 1921, Colonel C. K. Howard-Bury was leading the first expedition to climb the north side of Mount Everest when he saw dark shadows flitting over the slopes at 19,500 feet. Later, at the precise spot where he had seen the strange creatures, he found gigantic footprints.

What these dark figures wandering over the glacier slopes to the east of Mount Everest were nobody knew. But since the day of that sighting at such an extreme elevation, the stories surrounding a wild man of the snows have grown in number. The yeti has become Central Asia's most compelling mystery.

The great majority of the curious were more interested in promoting the yeti mystery than in solving it. Nobody cared what the people of the remote mountain valleys had to say. Instead, second- or thirdhand testimony would circulate, or film footage that had been gathering dust in Russian archives would surface, and later, videos taken by a group of tourists in the Himalayas. Yet nobody was ready to denounce these blurry images as fake. With the years, it became increasingly hard to tell what percentage of the sightings were bogus.

Slavomir Rawicz, a Polish cavalry officer who had managed to escape a Soviet prison camp in northern Siberia with a group of fellow convicts, describes encountering a yeti in his book *The Long Walk*. The men had made their way along the shores of Lake Baikal and then crossed the Gobi Desert. In March 1942, having managed to traverse the Himalayas, they descended the foothills into northern India, where they supposedly encountered the creatures, an encounter Rawicz describes as follows:

> In all our wanderings through the Himalayan region we had encountered no other creatures than man, dogs, and sheep. It was with quickening interest, therefore, that in the early stages of our descent of this last mountain, Kolomenos drew our attention to two moving black specks against the snow about a quarter of a mile below us. We thought of animals and immediately of food, but as we set off down to investigate we had no great hopes that they would await our arrival. The contours of the mountain temporarily hid them from view as we approached nearer, but when we halted on the edge of a bluff

we found they were still there, twelve feet or so below us and about a hundred yards away.

Two points struck me immediately. They were enormous and they walked on their hind legs. The picture is clear in my mind, fixed there indelibly by a solid two hours of observation. We just could not believe what we saw at first, so we stayed to watch. Somebody talked about dropping down to their level to get a close-up view.

Zaro said, "They look strong enough to eat us." We stayed where we were. We weren't too sure of unknown creatures which refused to run away at the approach of man.

I set myself to estimating their height on the basis of my military training for artillery observation. They could not have been much less than eight feet tall. One was a few inches taller than the other, in the relating of the

average man to the average woman. They were shuffling quietly around on a flatish shelf which formed part of the obvious route for us to continue our descent. We thought that if we waited long enough they would go away and leave the way clear for us. It was obvious they had seen us, and it was equally apparent they had no fear of us.

The American said that eventually he was sure we should see them drop on all fours like bears. But they never did.

Their faces I could not see in detail, but the heads were

squarish and the ears must lie close to the skull because there was no projection from the silhouette against the snow. The shoulders sloped sharply down to a powerful chest. The arms were long and the wrists reached the level of the knees. Seen in profile, the back of the head was a straight line from the crown into the shoulders—"like a damned Prussian," as Paluchowicz put it.

We decided unanimously that we were examining a type of creature of which we had no previous experience in the wild, in zoos, or in literature. It would have been easy to see them waddle off at a distance and dismiss them as either bear or big ape of the urang-outang species. At close range they defied facile description. There was something both of the bear and the ape about their general shape but they could not be mistaken for either. The color was a rusty kind of brown. They appeared to be covered by two distinct kinds of hair— the reddish hair which gave them their characteristic color forming a tight, close fur against the body, mingling with which were long, loose, straight hairs, hanging downwards, which had a slight grayish tinge as the light caught them.

Dangling our feet over the edge of the rock, we kept them closely under observation for about an hour. They were doing nothing but move around slowly together, occasionally stopping to look around them like people admiring a view. Their heads turned towards us now and again, but their interest in us seemed of the slightest.[1]

It wasn't until years later, when Rawicz studied the reports of a scientific expedition that had been sent out to look for traces of the "abominable snowman" and read about the descriptions by local inhabitants, that he became convinced he had seen two yetis.

Jan Frostis, a Norwegian uranium prospector, claimed to have encountered two yetis at Zemu Gap in the Sikkim Himalayas. One of them had attacked him and mauled his shoulder. The proof he offered was to some extent credible, but his story also had some dubious elements. He described the animal quite well, but his account in other respects was far-fetched. He and a fellow Norwegian named Thorberg were surveying the Zemu Glacier and had set up camp at Zemu Gap, a mountain pass located at 16,500 feet. One morning they found fresh footprints in the snow around their camp. Then they saw two dark spots far off in the distance. Through binoculars, the spots looked like people. Thorberg and Frostis ran after the figures and, when they got closer, realized they were yetis. "They walked upright and were more or less as big as humans. Their bodies were covered with rough, long-haired fur, but their faces were hairless and smooth."

They ensnared one of the creatures with a lasso that they had somehow managed to knot in the twinkling of an eye. The monster snapped the rope with one yank. Frostis describes how the creature then hurled itself at him, striking him a mighty blow. He fell to the ground, defenseless, a stinging pain in his shoulder. Apparently, Thorberg was armed and fired a shot, and the startled monster ran away.

It took Thorberg and some Sherpas a whole day to bring the wounded Frostis back to the camp. From there they carried him to a hospital in Darjeeling, where the Sherpas confirmed that a yeti had attacked him. Their testimony is the strongest element in the story—Frostis, after all, might have been attacked by wild animals—since for the Sherpas the yeti is a quasi-divine being and one does not mention it lightly.

When Eric Shipton took his world-famous picture of footprints in the snow of the Melung Glacier one November afternoon in 1951, it was thought that it offered final proof that the yeti existed. Shipton and his men followed the trail for about a mile, and it seemed as if the centuries' worth of tales and legends surrounding the yeti were about to become reality. The prints proved that whatever made them was enormous and heavy, that it walked on two feet, and that it lived in the glacial regions. Shipton's high-quality pictures clearly showed the long trail in the snow, and also the single footprint, oval in shape, over twelve inches long and very wide, with a protruding big toe. The photos made the yeti a legend in the West and an object of research for anthropologists, ethnologists, and zoologists.

Shipton's pictures did not shed light, however, on other aspects of the yeti mystery—the guttural whistles, the piercing shouts, the red hair, the strange nocturnal habits, the stones and branches thrown at travelers in the night. Questions remained unanswered, even after scientific laboratories had studied the photographs. One thing the pictures did manage to do was fan yeti hysteria. In the 1950s, searching for the yeti became the rage. Professional climbers went on search expeditions, as did weekend zoologists, reporters, and even a few serious scientists. Thrill-seeking in a world that had been almost fully explored drove them to new heights. When they did not find anything new, they began passing off fabrications as discoveries.

In those days there were more yeti expeditions than expeditions to conquer mountains over twenty-five thousand feet, a feat that had attracted public interest following the conquest of Mount Everest in 1953. In 1954, the editorial offices of *The Daily Mail* in London brought together an impressive group of experts for an expedition to Nepal. This expedition didn't find any yetis, but it did discover more footprints, dens, and even some fecal matter, which upon analysis proved that the creature that had made it was an omnivore. Like man, it was conjectured, the yeti fed on both animals and plants. The scientists concluded this creature didn't seem to be a bear, but more likely a descendant of *Gigantopithecus,* whose estimated height and build were strikingly similar to the creature that eyewitnesses described. As I've mentioned, remains of *Gigantopithecus* had been found in the foothills of the Himalayas, not too far from where yetis had been sighted. The mountain of speculation grew to new heights.

Tom Slick, a Texan oil millionaire who organized a yeti hunt in 1957, was told by Nepalese villagers that in the previous four years yetis had attacked villages, raided herds, and killed five people. He initiated a series of expeditions to the Himalayas, but in the end, frustrated by the lack of results, turned his attention to tracking down the Sasquatch—like the yeti and the Loch Ness monster, a creature of feverish speculation—back in America. He *had* to find something strange. The filmmaker Norman Dyhrenfurth, the son of mountain climber and geographer Gunther Oskar Dyhrenfurth, was, like his father, convinced that yetis existed. In 1958, he found footprints similar to the ones that Shipton had photographed, and in Arun he found what he described as the dens of apes or anthropoids.

During the same period, Squadron Leader L. W. Davies provided an account of his fascinating adventure farther south, in Lahul, although again he produced no evidence that the yeti was an anthropoid.

A little farther up the valley we came upon three large footprints on the edge of one of the snow islands that separated the meandering glacial streams to our right. A beast had evidently climbed out of the icy cold, swiftly running current onto the island. We tried to ford the stream but it was too cold and deep so we cast around to see where it had entered the water. We soon found that this was about a hundred yards upstream. From there we backtracked up the steep western side of the valley whence the beast had come, keeping clear of, but parallel to its tracks. It had walked steeply downhill on its hind legs and, where the gradient was too steep for walking, had slid on its behind. Careful examination had showed that it had used its fists, either to break or to assist its descent. The span between the left and the right fist-mark was about three yards. After measuring the dimensions of the footprints we trekked upstream to a snow bridge and returned along the far bank where, in due course, we reached the prints we had first seen. The water there was about 5 ft. deep—the current undercut the bank—and yet we could see no trace of forepaws or hands. Evidently, whatever it was that passed this way had been extremely tall and had simply stepped out of the deep water onto the edge of the island.

Like his fellow Ladakhis, Nawa Ram had previously scoffed at the anti-"yeti" precautions taken by our Sherpas. These had consisted of traps and mystical spinning tops made from base-camp debris. Now however his whole attitude changed.

"*Zarur Sahib, yeh balu nai hai,*" he exclaimed. "Certainly this is no bear."

The previous afternoon he had been assisting me with my cameras some 300 yards upstream and we found that our footprints had expanded by only one-eighth of an inch all round. The theory that "yeti" footprints are merely enlarged bear pug marks could therefore be ruled out in this case. Furthermore, since we had left the area at about 3:30 P.M. the previous day, we knew that the creature had crossed the valley between that time on June 11 and early the following morning. Close study of the prints on the island edge showed that it must have climbed out of the stream when the snow was freezing hard; that is, during the night or early morning.

During my previous six Himalayan seasons I had often seen black and red bears and their pug marks, but these prints in the Kulti were quite different. Each foot had five broad toes and the big toe was particularly prominent on some of the prints, which averaged 12 inches long and 8 inches wide. In places they had sunk 11 inches into the snow where my own boots, bearing over 14 stone, went in a mere 1½ inches beneath the noonday sun. Such deep impressions on hard snow indicate, therefore, a beast of great weight.

We spent several hours following the tracks, which extended for about half a mile. Our progress was made difficult by the numerous snow islands and icy cold streams. The beast had swum at least five of them before its tracks finally petered out on the rocky eastern wall of the valley. Nowhere had it

walked on all fours and the average pace between its footprints was nearly twice that of my own.

When we finally gave up the chase and returned to base
camp our Sherpas were convinced that we had seen the footsteps of a "yeti."[2]

In 1960, Sir Edmund Hillary himself led an expedition to the
borders of Nepal and Tibet in search of the yeti. The first leg of his
journey was to the spot where Shipton had taken his photos, in the
region below the peaks of Gauri Sankar and Menlungtse. The expedition carried state-of-the-art equipment for scientific analysis, as
well as an official Nepalese government decree prohibiting the capture or killing of a yeti, should one be found. But none were found.

Hillary's expedition did bring back furs that supposedly came
from yetis, and an abundance of photos of suspicious tracks in the
snow. They also managed to borrow the legendary "yeti scalp," a
relic housed in the Sherpa monastery of Khumjung. The furs
turned out to be from Tibetan bears. And the scalp, a stone-hard
leather cap with red bristles, was put under microscopes in laboratories in Chicago, Paris, and London and proved to be made from
the skin of a two-hundred-year-old wild Himalayan goat.

The expeditions of Edward W. Cronin and Dr. Howard Emery
in Kongmaa Laa in December of 1972 also turned out to be much
ado about nothing.

On the 17th, accompanied by two Sherpa assistants, Howard
and I emerged on a high alpine ridge connecting to Kongmaa Laa. The weather was beautiful, with a clear sky and
warm sun. The icy summit of Makalu dominated the horizon to the northwest. In the late afternoon, we discovered a
depression in the ridge at about 12,000 feet, a flat place with
firm snow that would be suitable for camp.

The area was small, less than half an acre, a completely
clear snowfield unmarked by animal prints. The slopes on the

side of the ridge were precipitous, falling several thousand feet to the Barun River on the north and the Kasuwa River on the south. We made camp, pitching two light tents, had dinner around an open fire, and retired just after dark. The evening was calm.

Shortly before dawn the next morning, Howard climbed out of our tent. Immediately, he called excitedly. There, beside the trail we had made to our tents, was a new set of footprints. While we were sleeping, a creature had approached our camp and walked directly between our tents. The Sherpas identified the tracks, without question, as yeti prints. We, without question, were stunned.

We immediately made a full photographic record of the prints before the sun touched them. Like the conditions Shipton had encountered, the surface consisted of crystalline snow, excellent for displaying the prints. These conditions were localized to our camp area and were the result of the effects produced on the depression by the sun and winds of earlier days. The prints were clearest in the middle of the depression, directly beside our trail, where some ten to fifteen prints, both left and right feet, revealed the details of the toes and general morphology of the creature's foot. Some of the right footprints were actually on our previous trail, making them difficult to interpret. Other prints of the right foot were distinct.

The prints measured approximately nine inches long by four and three-quarters inches wide. The stride, or distance between individual prints, was surprisingly short, often less than one foot, and it appeared that the creature had used a slow, cautious walk along this section. The prints showed a short, broad, opposable hallux, an asymmetrical arrangement of the toes, and a wide rounded heel. These features were present in all prints made on firm snow. Most impressively, their close resemblance to Shipton's prints was unmistakable.

We then proceeded to explore the rest of the trail left by the creature. By the direction of the toes on the clear footprints, I determined that the creature had come up the north slope. Because the north slope received less sun, it was covered by very deep snow, and the tracks consisted of large punch holes in the snow revealing little detail. I descended several hundred yards, but the heavy snow made walking impossible, and I was forced to cling to the slope with my hands. The creature must have been exceptionally strong to ascend this slope in these conditions. From a vantage point, I could look down the trail, which continued to the bottom of the valley in a direction generally perpendicular to the slope, but there seemed little advantage in climbing farther down, and I returned to the top of the ridge.

From our camp, the tracks continued out onto the south slope, but here the increased exposure to the sun had melted most of the snow, and there were bare patches of rock and alpine scrub which made following the trail extremely difficult. We walked farther up the ridge towards Kongmaa Laa to get a view of the trail from above, and discovered what appeared to be the prints of the same creature coming back onto the top of the ridge. They crossed back and forth several times. Here, the ridge was covered with low bushes, which enabled deeper snow to accumulate, and again the prints were confused punch holes. The trail then went back down onto the south slope, and attempted to follow but then lost the prints on the bare rock and scrub. The slope was extremely steep, and searching for the prints was arduous and dangerous. We realized that whatever creature had made them was far stronger than any of us.[3]

The avalanche of new stories surrounding the abominable snowman gained momentum with every passing year, and more and more people in the West conjured up an image of a monster somewhere between man and ape, based upon the jumble of eyewitness accounts, photographs, and plaster casts of footprints. As science was incapable of disproving that a gigantic anthropoid lived in the Himalayas, the yeti continued to be perceived as a close relative of man from the distant past. Everyone waited expectantly for explorers to come up with the most important zoological and anthropological discovery of the century, but they seemed less interested in solving the mystery than in gaining new insight into man's evolution, behavioral development, and the early forms of social interaction.

The descriptions of the yeti corresponded either to characteristics of fossilized anthropoids or to those of the ancient *Gigantopithecus*. Could an anthropoid the size of *Gigantopithecus* have survived undiscovered in the Himalayas? Even if yetis did cross the high mountain passes, which is where we found their footprints, in order to travel from one valley to another, they wouldn't be able to live up there indefinitely.

The more questions I asked the Sherpas and Tibetans in Katmandu, the more confused I became. Everyone I talked to confirmed that the yeti and the chemo were one and the same, but everyone had his own explanation for the enigma. Reading up on the yeti didn't get me any further either. To avoid being driven insane by this mystery, I would have to return to the mountains. One thing was certain: in the Himalayas lived a creature that had not yet been zoologically classified. Most believed that it was an unknown anthropoid that walked upright. I was increasingly convinced the yeti was an animal known to the Himalayan people since time immemorial, and one they considered a rival in their struggle for survival. The chemo might be a species of mutant bear, or a large type of ape, but it definitely was not a "wild man."

Those I spoke to in Katmandu knew the snowstorms of the high Himalayan passes as well as they knew the fiery sun of the Tibetan steppes. But nobody was sure which of the tales they recounted about the chemo and the yeti and which were fabrications. No one knew where one ended and the other began. They had grown up immersed in tales and superstitions—such as that the yeti was a harbinger of misfortune. This would not change even if I managed to solve the mystery. The yeti's power would never wane. Quite the opposite. The fewer that remained, the more they would grow in people's imaginations.

4

TALES OF THE YETI

A monsoon hovered over the Barun valley. A cold wind, tasting of fresh snow and decay, shook the walls of the brightly colored tents huddled near a stone hut. I walked past them over to the Sherpas' kitchen tent. Wafts of smoke and shreds of fog floated above the sparsely forested mountain meadows. We had set up camp for a few days to the southeast of Makalu.

Sakraman, our cook, offered me a plastic bottle filled with *rakshi,* which he took out of a basket of food supplies. With a gesture, he urged me to drink. I refused, thanking him, and a kitchen boy brought me some hot tea with milk.

"Every morning you climb up the rock face to the edge of the forest. What is it you're looking for in those hidden caves?" Sakraman asked me.

"A yeti," I answered, laughing.

"So you're one of those who believe that these man-apes live around here?"

"I don't believe anything. I'm just searching."

"He is looking for the last remnants of a breed of hominids with an incredible capacity for survival," Sabine—who had followed me to the kitchen tent—said sarcastically.

"Stop making fun of me!" I replied, smiling. Then I turned to Sakraman. "I want to hear what you Sherpas have to say."

"It's true that the yeti has been sighted most often in these parts in the past hundred years," Sakraman said.

"The wilderness between Makalu and Kanchenjunga is the perfect habitat," I added.

"But whenever the papers report that someone has seen the mysterious yeti, there's always something fishy."

"I also ask myself why in the reports the creature's height ranges from five feet to ten feet, the color of its fur fluctuates between reddish brown and dark brown, and that it is generally described as thickset with a short neck. Only its footprints suggest that this animal bears any resemblance to man, and that its arms are very long."

"Could a yeti be a man?" asked Sakraman.

"No, at least not a *Homo erectus*," I answered.

"How did the first men come about?"

"They say that about one and a half million years ago there were many species of hominid ape in Africa, and that one of these species developed into an ape that walked upright, the *Homo erectus*," I said.

"And these apes lived in families and could make fire and used hand axes as weapons?"

"So the textbooks say."

"Then these apes spread across the African continent, Asia, and Europe?"

"And here in the mountains they turned into yetis, while where I come from they turned into people."

Everyone laughed.

"Well, things didn't happen quite that quickly," I added. "With time the apes acclimatized themselves to the regions where they lived, but their intellectual development stagnated for well over a million years."

"So in the West you imagine the yeti is one of these humans at a lower stage of intellectual development?"

"Possibly."

"A preliminary stage to *Homo sapiens.*"

"Others in the West might believe this, but not me."

By this point we had been joined by other Sherpas, who listened intently to Sakraman and me talking. Sir Edmund Hillary had built schools in Solo Khumbu, and there the younger ones learned all sorts of subjects—geography, politics, zoology—and could discuss them with considerable sophistication.

"Many see the yeti as a creature at a primitive intellectual stage of development, similar to the one attributed to Neanderthals. But as rational, intelligent beings would we arrogant *Homo sapiens* have tolerated a Neanderthal for thirty-five thousand years? We became rulers of the world by rubbing out all the competition—at least until now."

"Is science still divided on this issue?" asked Sakraman.

"Zoologists and ethnologists have barely even focused on the yeti phenomenon. But everyone else—tourists, natives, and all the interested people around the world—are divided on this. The only concrete thing we have to go on are the footprints."

"Prints measuring one to one and a half feet."

"Yes," I replied. "Definitely too big for humans and anthropoids. Which means the yeti must belong to another species. And in some prints the instep is not discernible."

"Yetis are flat-footed?" asked Sakraman.

"No question."

"Footprints made in snow or damp, soft earth are easy to follow. This means autumn is the best time to track yetis."

"That's precisely why I'm on the lookout for them from early morning until late at night."

"And?"

"Well, nothing yet."

"I'm sure you'll find some tracks tomorrow."

"Maybe ones you made," I rejoindered.

Sakraman laughed.

"I can tell real ones from fake ones right away," I said. "The fake ones look stiff and unnatural."

"Have they actually found real footprints?"

"They've even taken pictures of them."

"But why do these tracks suddenly stop?"

I shrugged my shoulders. "No idea."

"Maybe yetis can fly."

"What?"

"Just an idea," Sakraman added. "Why couldn't a yeti be a bird? I love imagining how great it would be to fly from one camp to the next."

Later that evening, I asked Sakraman how many Himalayan expeditions he had been on.

"About seventy," he answered. "But in ten years I'll be too old, and in twenty I might die. That's why I wish I could fly."

"And you think the yeti can?" I asked after a moment of silence.

"They say he doesn't need sleep and can live off air alone. Why shouldn't he be able to fly, too?"

"What man can't do, the yeti can?"

"At least, I think so."

The people of the Himalayas don't tend to be overly curious. Once the facts about the yeti ran dry, they simply began inventing, and they lied to tourists on principle. Scientists from all over the world had spun together more than a hundred names for an as yet undiscovered creature—about which the Sherpas kept spinning new tales while sitting around their campfires.

My Sherpa cook was no teller of tall tales, however. He lived the simple life of his tribe. Back in Solo Khumbu he subsisted on the fruits of the earth, yaks, and barley. The only money he earned was as a cook on expeditions.

Listening carefully to what the Sherpas say, I began to discern three types of yeti. There was the gigantic, gluttonous *dzu teh,* which is almost eight feet tall when standing on its hind legs, reeks, and is nocturnal. He tends to walk on all fours and resembles the Tibetan bear. Secondly, there was the *thelma,* a smaller, apelike creature that walks upright and has long, dangling arms. Its fur is generally reported to be red or light brown, and its description matches that of the Assamese gibbon, which has been known to stray into the forests of northern Nepal. And finally there was the *mih teh,* an apelike creature the size of a man that allegedly has red fur on its face and stomach, and which sometimes attacks humans. The anthropoid-like *mih teh* is the one depicted in religious scrolls and on monastery walls.

I never quite understood whether the Sherpas consider this *mih teh* to be a yeti. They never offer conclusive explanations for any of the three types. When Sherpas are shown pictures of animals and asked which they think is a yeti, they usually point to orangutans. Because fossils of extinct giant orangutans have been found near the foothills of the Himalayas, this gives a certain relevance to the answer. Did the orangutans live there before man? Whatever the answer, none of these giant apes would have been capable of surviving in the snow regions, or even just below them.

If yetis weren't extinct but, as I believed, hovering on the brink of extinction, then all three Sherpa definitions of the *yeh teh* were apt. The three yeti types, I decided, had to be referring to one animal at different stages of development: older animals were larger and darker than younger ones, omnivores, and constantly on the run. As yetis were nocturnal, it shouldn't surprise us that local people who encounter them in the night might find it difficult to provide specifics.

I didn't find any signs of the yeti on our trek to Makalu, and though I was disappointed, I wasn't much surprised. There have never been any sightings in the glacial terrain. Tibetans living in the border regions have climbed the twenty-thousand-foot passes to cross over into Nepal and back. Nawang Tenzing, one of the strongest porters, once told me that as a child he had been sent to Nepal alone, tied to the back of a yak. Friends of the family had then taken him to Namche Bazar. Nawang Tenzing often told me tales about the yeti (and when he did, he would always parody the fearful expression of the lamas, who would put on yeti furs to scare each other).

In Solo Khumbu, where I headed right after my Makalu climb, two yeti scalps could be found—one in the Pangboche monastery and the other in Namche Bazar. The Pangboche monastery also housed the bones of a yeti hand. These relics were evidently fakes, like the furs of Rongbuk. Most Sherpas, however, believed they were real.

More recent yeti tales that the Sherpas told me sounded plausible. In 1974, a Sherpa girl was abducted by an "anthropoid" in Machermo; people heard high-pitched whistles beforehand. When the police came, they found two yaks with broken spines. A little later, a Japanese camp and a Polish base camp were attacked by an animal that left strange footprints in the snow. Members of the expedition followed the trail to take pictures and ran up against a snarling animal the likes of which they had never before seen. Again, none of them provided conclusive evidence.

The yeti has always manifested itself in the fantasy of the Sherpas as legend and reality: a snowman and a demon all in one, a mixture of fairy tale, reality, and nightmare. My only interest was finding out whether a bear or an ape hid behind the illusion. I had ruled out a prehistoric man.

One thing above all had become clear to me: the yeti story is linked to very different concerns in the Himalayas than in Europe. In the West, the single most compelling aspect of the yeti is its relation to the larger story of how we became human. Whether or not this has been so since the beginning of our history, as our millennium draws to a close, the issue goes to the heart of our culture. Evolutionary biologists have probed the mysteries of our origins and our creation, but many remain unsatisfied with their conclusions. Might there not, some wonder, be some completely different, unconventional, and speculative answers to the question of man's origins? It is this quest for an explanation that has kept the yeti legend alive in the West. In other words, the yeti has directed our curiosity backward. For the people of the Himalayas, it contributes to daily reality. Their yeti is a presence. They love talking of a creature that has a habit of eating and drinking from containers left as little a hundred yards from camps or settlements. (Of course, that shouldn't make it difficult to study and photograph one.) But why is misfortune predicted for a whole village when a yeti is sighted or when a yeti relic disappears from a monastery?

The myth of the yeti will survive for as long as the natives imagine it as more than just an animal. The tales fulfill longings and dreams—such as Sakraman's dream of flying—and fears, and provide the awe of something with superior power.

I would have loved to have seen dignitaries from the Tengpoche monastery dance about the temple grounds. But it was fall, and the Mani Rimdu celebrations—with their yeti dances—are held in spring. During the celebrations monks wear stylized yeti masks, and one of them even dons a yeti scalp. The yeti is represented as something between a bear and an ape, and the fur of the yeti scalp is normally a rusty brown. What could be more natural for the audience than to equate snowman and demon?

When Sabine and I returned to Katmandu, we found that Tarchen, our Tibetan interpreter, had also returned. In the fifties, Tarchen had belonged to the Tibetan resistance. Whole monastic communities had tried to halt the advance of the Chinese army, which was spraying their monasteries with bullets.

"A group of us found a dead yeti behind a rock. The Chinese

had shot him," Tarchen told me when I asked him if he had ever seen a chemo.

"And how do you know it really was a yeti?"

"He looked just like a man."

"What about his fur?"

"They had skinned him. And his skinned body looked just like that of a man—maybe bigger and more muscular, but just like that of a man."

Tarchen was a friend of mine, and I had the deepest respect for him. He had achieved through hard work a degree of prosperity in Katmandu and lived there happily with his family. He had a store in Tamel, a carpet workshop, and a house near the airport. In his way he did all he could to keep alive the memory of the world on the other side of the Himalayas. He spoke incessantly of Tibet, and of the melting snows and the chemo, all of which, after the decades of homesickness and persecution, belonged together in his mind. In Nepal he was always doing his best to help other Tibetan refugees, if only by reminding them of what was happening in Tibet. He spoke of overcrowded cities, ruined monasteries, and a vanquished people. To older exiled Tibetans clinging to life in the hope that they might someday return to Tibet, he was particularly attentive. Where there was no hope, there could be no home.

Tarchen told others of my yeti encounter as if he had experienced it himself. He was sure one could find yetis in eastern Tibet. Through him, my quest became the talk of the town, spreading beyond the houses of the Tibetan refugees and Sherpas. Soon the streets of Katmandu were abuzz with rumors of it. These rumors were increasingly blown out of proportion and eventually spilled over into a press conference organized after I had conquered Makalu and Lhotse, two eight-thousand-meter mountains I climbed in succession in the fall of 1986.

Toward the end of the conference an Indian journalist raised the issue. "Is it true," he asked, "that you encountered a yeti during your Makalu expedition?"

I hesitated.

"Could you please confirm or refute this information?" he insisted.

"It wasn't during my Makalu expedition," I replied. "It was in Tibet."

My words created an uproar. I added, "But this has nothing to do with what we're talking about."

"So did you see a yeti, yes or no?" The Indian wanted a definite answer.

"Yes, but I do not wish to comment any further on this matter."

When I saw the newspapers the following day, I couldn't believe my eyes. The news of my conquering the last two of the fourteen eight-thousanders I had climbed in my life was lost among yeti hysteria, jeering comments, and absurd speculation. Calls began coming in from all over the world. Everyone wanted to know about the yeti. Nobody was interested that I had just returned from the Sherpa territories and the Barun region, where scientific expeditions had spent years searching for the yeti. Were yetis still living in the central Himalayas, they would have to be in the side valleys of the Arun Valley, where there had been repeated sightings of footprints. All that people wanted was for me to confirm that I had seen what they imagined the yeti to be. Nothing else mattered.

Only when I returned to Europe did I realize to what extent my words had been misunderstood. Self-proclaimed yeti experts declared me insane. More upsetting, some fellow climbers seemed to think that my search for the yeti was a publicity stunt. What they didn't understand was that I would have generated much more effective publicity for myself by ignoring the yeti question when it came up. What climber would be foolish enough to compromise his greatest climbing achievement with some vague comment about a yeti encounter? The story had hit the press because I had let my guard down for a few moments and answered spontaneously. All I had wanted to express was my hope to get to the bottom of the mystery.

Back home in Austria, I was shocked to read in the papers accusations that I must have been hallucinating in the Himalayas and, oxygen-deprived, had seen yetis in the cloud formations. Zoology experts declared that what I had encountered was a Himalayan black bear. A slew of yeti jokes had begun making the rounds.

It was easier to come up with yeti jokes than with concrete evidence proving or disproving their existence.

I got wind of a story that sounded so improbable that I even began doubting my own encounter. Two professors named Porshnev and Mashkovtsev, both members of the Soviet Academy of Sciences, had investigated the story of Zana, a female yeti who was said to have lived in the Caucasus. Zana had been captured and tamed and, for many years, had lived in the village of Tkhina, where she was said to have died around 1890. One of the oldest villagers still remembered her in 1962, and everybody in Tkhina was certain she had existed. Seventy-two years after her death, Zana's tale was still being told.

It would seem that Zana "belonged" to Edgi Genaba, an aristocratic landowner who kept her locked up in a sturdy pen. At first she behaved like a wild animal, but over time she became tamer. Eventually she was allowed to roam free and slept out in the open, as she couldn't bear the warmth of the rooms in Genaba's house. When the children in the village taunted her with sticks, she chased them away by hurling stones. People said that she could run faster than a horse over short distances. Her body was gigantic and covered with reddish hair, and she had enormous breasts, muscular arms, and fingers that were much longer and thicker than human fingers. Her skin was black or dark brown, and the black hair on her head was shaggy and shiny. Zana could not speak, but she could communicate with noises and had excellent hearing. By all accounts, her face was frightening: it was broad, with high cheekbones and a flat nose; her eyes had a reddish tint. Zana was taught simple household chores, such as grinding corn and gathering firewood, and as the years passed she lived more and more among people.

Zana became pregnant with human children, according to the story. She gave birth without a midwife and immediately took her infants to the river to wash them in the freezing water, which killed them. Four of her children, however—two sons and two daughters—were taken away by the villagers the moment they were born and grew up to be normal human beings. They were intelligent, able to speak, and were completely assimilated into local society. They all had children of their own. Khvit, Zana's youngest son, died in 1954.

What intrigued me about the story, despite its inconsistencies, was how close it was to other yeti legends. A hominid creature turns up, its appearance and behavior that of an animal's, and in just one generation it makes a successful developmental leap to modern man. Since she bore human children, Zana's genetic code must have been compatible with that of a human being.

Although taken seriously by distinguished Soviet scientists, the tale of Zana is too grotesque to be factual. It asks instead to be read as an allegory. Zana represents the leap from animal to human, and her story mirrors human evolution. Her tale does not prove that the gene structures of modern humans were mixed with those of a primitive hominid; it merely proves that people all over the world seek answers to the same questions. And when science offers them no proof, they turn to myths.

A flood of letters from would-be yeti explorers provided me with additional proof of my theory. One woman sent me her yeti drawings, asking whether she had captured its likeness. An ethnologist specializing in the Himalayas wrote that in 1970 he had had a nocturnal encounter with a creature his Sherpas identified as a yeti. He offered to help get me an introduction to the Rongbuk Gompa monastery, where the monks were known to have "friendly relations" with yetis.

In 1987, when I was on a lecture tour, the British newspaper *The Telegraph* ran an item about a climbing team from the Jammu and Kashmir Departments of Nature Conservation. They had apparently traveled to the village of Hewan, forty miles from Srinagar, where a member of the team, sixteen-year-old Mushtaq Ahmend Khan, got into a fight with a brown-haired, manlike creature believed to have been a yeti.

Why, I wondered, did yeti experts always surface when there was a story—particularly one in which a yeti kidnaps somebody—only to disappear again once things calmed down? True stories tend to survive the passage of time. Over a hundred years ago Paul Belloni du Chaillu, a French-American explorer, was the first to shoot a gorilla, an animal that for two thousand years Europeans had believed to be mythical. At first, the public reacted with mocking disbelief to the news. Many years passed before the existence of the gorilla was accepted in Europe.

Why this skepticism? The answer is simple enough: explorers and discoverers see what they want to see. Like all of us, they perceive reality through their preconceptions. They take what locals tell them back home to Europe and America, where the stories are lapped up by the eager masses. And because most of us are busy trying to figure out who *we* are, the yeti inevitably ends up being more than just an animal. We endow it with "hands" and "feet"; it drifts through the world of our imagination, endowed with a consciousness similar to our own. As most of us hope the yeti will fit into a chain of evolution that we like to think has a purposeful and rational progression—regardless of what supernatural power set it off—the yeti has to be more than a mere bear or ape. Perceiving it as an anthropoid superior to us in strength but inferior in intellect caters to our dream that the world is made for man.

Self-proclaimed yeti experts ignore that the number of anthropoid species has drastically diminished since mankind evolved from one of them, and that the chances that there are other beings in the universe with our form of intelligence are practically nil. Flights of fancy have fed the legend for over a century, and the world's craving for the esoteric overpowers the evidence.

Having by then spent half a year focusing on the yeti, I realized that two tasks lay before me: first, to find why the yeti legend had developed and endured in so many different, unconnected places, from Pamir to the eastern Himalayas; and second, to convince the world that there was a living creature behind the legend, and that it was called a chemo. I could only succeed at these two tasks by returning to the places where the legends had sprung up and by observing the chemo in its habitat. Neither Tibetan exiles nor Western scientists would help me solve the mystery. I needed to seek the mountain people who conceived of the abominable snowman as part of their world, not an invention.

Further research in Katmandu among Tibetan exiles was useless. The monsters, spirits, and other specters they had brought with them into exile had not been forgotten, but their mythical potential had been lost. Years in India, or Los Angeles, or in a Tibetan monastic village in Switzerland had affected their memories. Every time they told their tales, their chemos became Indian, American, or European.

5

GODS AND DEMONS

My quest was putting me in the spotlight.

"Here comes the yeti!" teenagers would shout after me in the street back home in Austria—or they would block my path, point at my chest, and grunt, "You yeti?"

Everywhere I went I was asked the same question: What do yetis look like? I sometimes ignored the question, particularly when it was posed by grinning skeptics hoping to embarrass me. But sometimes I let myself get involved in conversations I realized must have sounded surreal.

Here's an example:

"What kind of an image of the yeti should we Europeans have?" was the first question a journalist who had come to see me at my home, Schloss Juval, asked.

"You have to forget about the European yeti," I replied.

"Why's that?"

"The yeti is just a joke here."

"So you're really going to search for this mythical creature?"

"No, of course not. How can you expect me to find a mythical creature? There is one thing that I know for certain: the yeti legend is tied in with a specific, if rare, species of animal."

"Does that mean that the yeti isn't an abominable snowman?"

"What you call the abominable snowman doesn't really exist."

"You mean it's a false interpretation?"

"When the Himalayan people talk about the yeti, they are referring to two rare species of animal, which according to zoology are probably extinct."

"This is getting more and more complicated."

"If it were simple, we wouldn't be arguing. What I intend to do is prove that only one species corresponds to the Nepalese, and more specifically the Tibetan, yeti legend. I also intend to prove that these animals have survived to this day."

"You mean you are going to give us an animal?"

"That is the only way I can reveal the truth behind the yeti legend. The only thing that interests me is the link between this particular animal and the stories surrounding the yeti."

"So you are not searching for the abominable snowman?"

"No. I repeat: I'm searching for the animal that gave rise to the yeti legend."

"Why has no one done this before?"

"Because, I believe, no one was looking for the right thing."

"What you're saying is, they were looking for the yeti but not for what gave rise to the legend?"

"Everyone was looking for an abominable snowman, a Neanderthal, or something like that. Without much success, needless to say."

"How do you intend to prove the creature's zoological origins?"

"If I manage to observe the animal and to photograph and film it, I would have conclusive evidence about the yeti. That is, if its

appearance and behavior were compatible with those of the mythological creature."

"The yeti will no longer be an imaginary creature?"

"Well, yes and no. Should I manage to photograph the animal,
then I will prove that the yeti is a combination of legend and reality."

"I see you are obsessed with this idea."

"I wouldn't say that. I'm just working intensely on it."

"Exclusively?"

"No, I am also pursuing other projects. I'm planning to go to the
South Pole, a trip that is very important to me. Ten years from now
I'll no longer be able to make it there, but I might still be able to
photograph a yeti."

"Could your position on the yeti cost you your credibility?"

"That depends."

"On whether people believe you or not?"

"It's not a question of believing. The skeptics will hang on to
their ideas for quite a while."

"Why?"

"The more naive among them believe all the bizarre yeti tales
going around. They might well be disappointed by what I find.
They want the stories to be true."

"And those less naive?"

"They might initially ridicule my findings,
but I hope they will come to see that the yeti
stories are a combination of reality and myth.
And someday, maybe decades from now,
when anthropologists will have established
that the zoological yeti is different from
the mythical one, the word *yeti* will finally
describe something closer to reality."

"What role does the yeti play in
Tibetan religion?"

"That's an interesting and important

question. Long before the yeti became a known entity in the West, it was an important part of the religious life of the Himalayan people. In the rituals of the ancient shamanistic Bön religion, for instance, which was widespread in Tibet before the advent of Lamaism, yeti blood and yeti scalps were part of the ritual sacrifices. The blood of a yeti or 'wild man' was mixed with that of a horse, a dog, a goat, a pig, a raven, a human, or a Himalayan bear. The ritual demanded that the blood of the yeti be obtained by killing it with arrows."

"Are there still such ceremonies today?"

"Yes, during the Mani Rimdu Festival in the monastery of Khumjung, beneath Mount Everest, I observed a man wearing a sheepskin and a conical replica of a yeti scalp. He carried a bow and arrow. And something else, too—supposedly there is a curse on the actor who performs this hunter role. The ritual is practiced according to written instructions that have been handed down, even if the meaning of all the symbols is obscure."

"So is the yeti some sort of deity?"

"Perhaps a deity and a demon. But no one in the West can hope to understand all of the yeti's religious implications."

My interviewer remained skeptical. "I wonder," he asked hesitatingly, "if an ape similar to the orangutan managed to survive in the Himalayas?"

"No, I'm sure that's impossible."

"I think that the yeti is an imagined creature that sprang from peoples' collective unconscious."

"I don't. First of all, mankind needs some sort of model when it invents its monsters. And then, don't forget, I saw one of these animals."

"Could this yeti have been a hallucination?"

"Do you mean because of the thin atmosphere? No. Up there, where the yetis live, neither Tibetans nor Sherpas suffer from a lack of oxygen."

The longer we discussed the yetis, the wilder the illusions the journalist entertained.

"Stop guessing," I finally said in exasperation. "Stop imagining. Travel to Tibet and you'll understand better. You will only get at the root of the yeti story by getting far away from libraries and editorial offices. Here we can only speculate—badly."

After this interview, I, too, resolved to stop speculating about the yeti. My search had to begin by questioning obvious facts and opening myself up to the strange and mysterious. The truth about the yeti would be found far away from Western sensationalism.

Later, I showed my interviewer two texts that discussed the yeti's religious significance. The first was *The Life and Teachings of the Masters of the Far East* by Baird Spalding, and the second *Heart of Asia* by Nicholas Roerich, an artist and ascetic who had visited the Himalayas and its people in the 1920s.

Spalding, who had gone on a three-and-a-half-year exploratory expedition to the Himalayas, had this to say about the yeti:

> They are God's children, the same as we are, only they have lived so long in hatred and fear of their fellow-men, and they have so developed the hatred and fear faculty that they have isolated themselves from their fellow-men to such an extent that they have completely forgotten they are descendants of the human family, and think themselves the wild creatures they appear to be. They have gone on this way until they have even lost the instinct of the wild creatures, for the wild creatures knows by instinct when a human loves it and it will respond to that love. All we can say is, that man brings forth that which he gazes upon, and separates himself from God and man, and in this way he can go lower than the animal.[4]

Roerich quotes *The Statesman,* India's leading newspaper of the time, which had published an account of the adventures of a British major:

Once before sunrise while camping in the Himalayas, the major went from his camp to the neighboring cliffs to see the majestic snowcapped outlines of the mountains. On the opposite side of the gorge rose a high rock. Great was his astonishment when through the morning mist he noticed on the rock the figure of a tall man, almost naked and with long black hair. The man was leaning on a high bow, attentively watching something behind the rock. Then, apparently noticing something, the silent figure, with great strides, leaped down the almost vertical slope. Completely amazed, the major returned to the camp and asked the servants about this strange apparition. But to his utter surprise, they took it quite calmly and with reverence told him: "Sahib has seen one of the snowmen, who guard the forbidden region."[5]

How difficult it is to separate credible accounts from incredible ones. Accounts by Westerners—Russians, Englishmen, or Germans—are more often than not invented, badly researched, and of little interest to me, even the hair-raising novels. But reports by locals also seemed problematic. Was that, I wondered, because the local population was not sufficiently knowledgeable about Himalayan wildlife? More likely is that Sherpas and the Tibetans often do not separate their reality from their religion, which is endlessly rich in myths, gods, and demons. Regardless of whether the yeti appears as a damned spirit, a thieving monster, or a protector of monasteries and mountains—in Tibetan, *playing yeti* means both "to protect" and "to rob"—it is omnipresent. I found it particularly interesting that in depictions of the cosmos, the yeti is pictured above animals but below humans. On the scrolls that serve as meditation aids in the monasteries, the yeti is positioned between animals and mankind.

For over a century, there have been rumors that yeti mummies were being kept in remote Tibetan monasteries. These mummies would be ideal for classifying yetis zoologically. After all, a dead specimen is less likely to elude scientific scrutiny than one living somewhere in the dark depths or blinding heights of the Himalayas. How, I wondered, was it possible that to date no explorer, trekker, or climber had come across one of these mummies, which were thought to reside in monasteries located in Riwoche, a region in eastern Tibet?

Lama Chhemed Riglizin Dorje Lopen, who fled to India after the Chinese ousted the Dalai Lama, revealed a secret from a West Tibetan monastery. Lama Lopen often visited the Sakya Monastery near Shigatse and became close to the head monk, who allowed him to enter the secret catacombs where many famous Tibetan lamas and scholars lay in sarcophagi. In one of the chambers of the catacombs he came upon a mummy and was told that four more of them were in the cellars of the monastery. The monks whispered to him that inside lay the "uncatchable ice man," yet another name for the yeti in Tibet. He beheld a shriveled-up creature lying on its side, completely mummified. The body was well enough preserved for him to conclude that it was that of a giant ape.

If this report is true, the yeti has played a far more important role in Tibetans' religious life than previously thought.

King Trisongdetsen, who ruled Tibet between 755 and 797, invited the Indian yogi Padma-Sambhava to Tibet to aid in the reintroduction of Buddhism. The yogi oversaw the building of the monasteries in Samye, thereby contributing to the suppression of the Tibetan Bön religion. The result of Padma-Sambhava's efforts was the establishment of a deeply esoteric form of Tibetan Buddhism. Elements of Bön remained intact. This was the foundation for Tibetan culture, in which spiritual elements blend with aspects of shamanism.

Tibetans claim to be descendants of a monkey god, an incarnation of Tshenrezig. Legend has it that Tshenrezig married a demon, who bore him six children with long hair and tails. They were fed anointed grains until their hair and tails began shriveling away and then dropped off completely. According to the ancient texts, some of these children inherited their father's qualities, others those of their mother—"but they were all mighty and brave."

In the Sherpa version of this legend, an ape who converts to Buddhism lives as a hermit in the mountains, then marries a demon. Their offspring are yetis, also with tails and long hair—anthropoids from the land of the snows. The yeti, in other words, was a Buddhist!

This idea fits the theory of a Nepal zoologist named Kaiser, who argued that yetis might be escaped convicts who fled into the mountains to evade the Tibetan police or Chinese and Indian gangsters, or possibly monks belonging to a remote Tibetan monastery unknown to the outside world. In some cases monks have taken vows to never again communicate with the outside world and rigorously adhered to these vows.

Many Sherpas also believe that yetis are the bodyguards of Dölma, the female incarnation of Tshenrezig. These guards embody the animistic deities from the pre-Buddhist religion, which envisioned the possibility that a person's soul might transfer to the body of lower anthropoids, and hence why in part yetis are venerated by some sects. Animistic beliefs still play a part in some of their rituals. Mummies, hands, and scalps are kept as proof of the existence of gods and demons, though from a zoological standpoint, they have nothing to do with the yeti.

When Sabine and I set out on a trip to Bhutan in the early summer of 1987 with a small group of friends, I knew that all these religious aspects would not by themselves help me solve the yeti mystery, but without being familiar with them I would never have understood the perspective of the local people. The religious context was what had turned the chemo—were it to turn out to be an animal—into the mythological yeti.

By 1987, the small and isolated kingdom of Bhutan, located between China and India, had been open to tourists for only a decade. Professor Franz Rhomberg, the physician to the late king, introduced us to Bhutan society in the capital, Thimphu, completely closed off to the rest of the world.

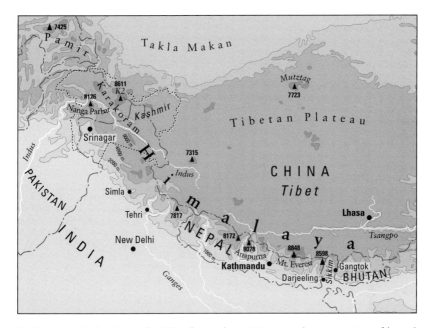

In the countries bordering the Himalayas, the yeti is more than a creature of legend.

I encountered my first yeti near this ravine in 1986.

OPPOSITE, TOP:
The footprint that started me on my quest for the yeti.

OPPOSITE, BOTTOM:
A fresh footprint in the mud next to young barley plants.

RIGHT: *A yak nomad.*

BELOW: *A Tibetan woman talking with Sabine in Lhasa.*

The Potala Palace in Lhasa, once the seat of the Dalai Lama, is now a museum.

I have met with the 14th Dalai Lama on numerous occasions and discussed the yeti, among other topics.

The Tengpoche Monastery in the Himalayan Sherpa lands.

A yeti dancer at the Mani Rimdu Festival.

A so-called yeti scalp from the monastery of Pangboche.

A stamp from the Kingdom of Bhutan, depicting the yeti as a kind of Himalayan King Kong.

A snow lion, an imaginary Tibetan heraldic beast.

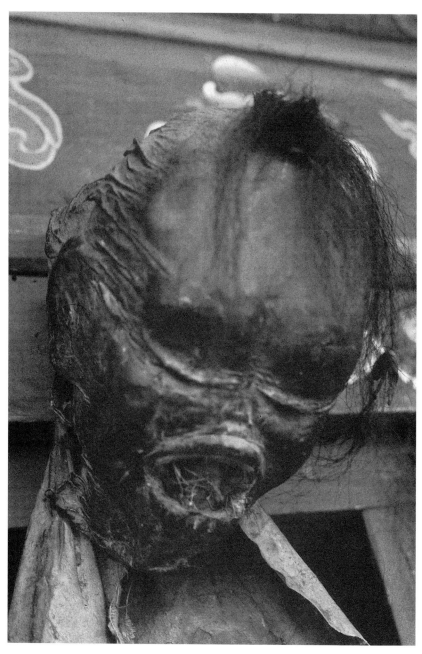

ABOVE AND OPPOSITE: *The mummy of what I was told was a yeti cub hidden in a Bhutanese monastery. An inspection of its scalp proved it to be fake.*

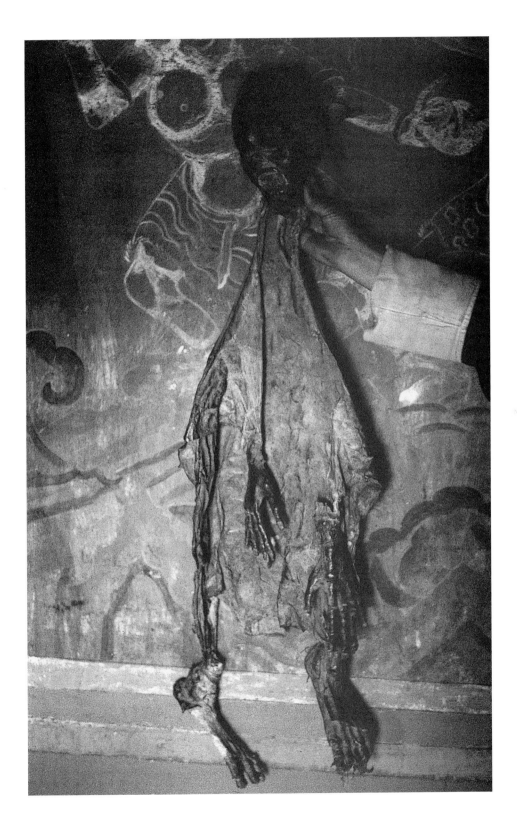

A Tibetan black bear in the Norbulinka Zoo in Lhasa.

OPPOSITE, TOP: *A chemo in captivity. I became convinced that this rare species was the basis for the yeti legend.*

OPPOSITE, BOTTOM: *A chemo paw.*

A few chemos still live in the forests behind this Lama monastery.

OPPOSITE, TOP: *Nochar, a hunter and chemo expert, accompanied me on my 1997 trip to Kham.*

OPPOSITE, BOTTOM: *This chemo den, insulated with hay and leaves, is located only about an hour's walk from the nearest settlement.*

*I photographed the entrance to this monastery in Kham in 1997. The stuffed
yak and "yeti" were hanging over the main entrance to the gompa, the monk's prayer
room, as if to ward off unwanted visitors.*

Two men holding a stuffed chemo near a monastery.

In a ritual dance, the stuffed chemo becomes the yeti.

After a few days in Thimphu, we headed west across narrow gorges toward the borders of Tibet, where I hoped to find traces of the yeti. There are only five passes between the steep glacial mountains through which one can cross into Tibet in summer. The Bhotias, Bhutanese of Tibetan origin, had originally crossed these passes. The slopes above the cleared areas were covered with forests, and the foothills looked as if they were coated with thick green fur. There were bears, tigers, and snakes, and during the monsoons leeches fell from the trees by the thousands.

It was May, and at first our small horse caravan made good progress. The tangy aroma of sage followed us as we traveled the centuries-old trails that led over the pine-covered mountain slopes. Higher up, we loaded our bags onto yaks and visited summer settlements where I asked the locals about yetis. I have always loved sitting in smoky huts and sleeping under the open sky. When the first monsoons came, we took refuge behind the stone walls of Lingshi Dzong, a monastic fortress now in ruins.

It rained constantly as we trekked back to Thimphu. The sublimeness of the Himalayas was replaced by damp tents and drenched ponchos. A sea of fog lay beneath us, with only an odd scrap of forest visible. The sky, too, was mostly gray, and just when it began clearing, new clouds rolled in, fast and ominous, making us feel trapped in the desolate terrain. The expedition ended without my having seen much of the mysterious forests of Bhutan, let alone any yetis.

Back in the half-timbered houses of the tilled valleys, I learned more about how bears and apes in this part of the world were perceived as harbingers of misfortune. But I learned nothing about the yeti or chemo, even in the whitewashed monastic fortresses with their colorful window banners, the spiritual, political, and administrative power centers of the country. I did find a postage stamp with a depiction of a yeti, but it seemed more of a joke than anything else. Photographs of the young leader of Bhutan, known as the Dragon King, hung everywhere—in the living rooms of the elite, the offices of local officials, and the dining rooms of tourist accommodations, constant reminders to both natives and visitors of the dynasty that has ruled the country since the beginning of the century.

Later that summer Sabine and I flew to Pakistan to talk about the yeti with the Kalash people, who live far up in the northern part of the country. We reached Peshawar, the capital of the area. Even after a sixteen-hour bus ride we still hadn't reached our goal, which was the town of Chitral. The road north was impassable because of bad weather, and on foot it would have been a three-day trek to the Hindu Kush. We would have had to cross two high passes that were deeply snowed in. A group of about thirty tried to make this crossing. We waited for two days for news of whether they had made it, then decided to leave, taking a more northern route that climbed sharply into the Hindu Kush. It started to snow on the first day, so we sought refuge in one of the rickety hovels that we found along the road.

There I met a shepherd named Mohammed Khan, who told me of an encounter he'd had with a strange creature the previous winter. One evening, just after sunset, he thought he saw a yeti near his goat pen.

"What did he look like?" I asked him.

"I couldn't see his face in the dark, and then suddenly he was gone."

"Do you think he looked more like an ape or a bear?" I asked.

"Neither. More like a man. He walked on two feet, upright, hunched slightly forward."

"What about his color?"

"He had dark skin, hair everywhere."

Khan wouldn't say more. I wondered if he wasn't merely repeating some tale he'd heard. Everyone in the Hindu Kush knows of the yeti. The Udshur call it *baman* in their language; in Chitani it is called *jangal mosh,* which basically means "human." But as was the case in Nepal, Tibet, and Sikkim, I would have to climb higher into the mountains to find answers.

After we'd finished our conversation and drunk our tea, we set off again, encountering a group of men coming down from the mountains carrying a stretcher. On it was a dead man. We stopped for a moment in shock. Then we continued walking up the road until we came to a bend, where a group of people, mostly men, were standing around a low litter made of wood and wickerwork. On it was another corpse. An old man was sobbing, the others stood in silence. I joined the group of men and found out that the people who had set out for Chitral had been struck by an avalanche. Nobody knew how many of them had been engulfed. They were still looking for survivors.

Sabine and I looked at each other. Our trip to Chitral and the valley of the Kalash, even our search for the yeti, no longer seemed important. There was too much snow in the Hindu Kush, and a war was being fought in neighboring Afghanistan. We packed our bags and left for home.

6

AMONG

THE YAK NOMADS

I returned to Lhasa in 1988, and even within the space of two years much had changed, principally because of the building frenzy of the Chinese. The Potala Palace, once at the edge of the city, was now in its center. The outskirts of town still looked like a refugee camp, with nomads and mountain dwellers setting up their tents and herding their livestock along the roads. Garbage was still piled high on the sidewalks.

Within Potala Palace were countless Buddha figures and sacrificial offerings, symbolizing the ephemeral nature of the body. The streets below were jammed with traffic. The kites of Tibetan children frequently got tangled up in the electric wires. There was no longer any sign of the human spirit's journey toward reincarnation.

A calendar and a clock in the fourteenth Dalai Lama's former bedroom, which had remained untouched since his flight on March

17, 1959, indicated when the old world had vanished. I wondered if the yeti had vanished with it.

In Norbulinka, the Dalai Lama's former summer palace located on the outskirts of Lhasa and once a place of retreat for the god-kings, Chinese and Tibetans were having picnics and playing *sbag,* a game similar to dominoes. The zoo was in disrepair, and I searched in vain for the animals—some said they were chemos—that had supposedly once been kept there. I wondered whether the Dalai Lama remembered them.

Were "chemo meat" and herbal brew still being used for medicinal purposes? Where were the yeti mummies kept hidden? Would the Chinese authorities allow me to travel to the mountains southeast of Amdo?

The Chinese paid no attention to tourists, and the Tibetans seemed preoccupied with mumbling their prayers, as they had done for centuries. Traditionally, prayers were written on strips of paper, then rolled into cylinders and stuffed into containers the size of a fist. These were set in motion by a swipe of the hand; a weight revolving around a metallic rod in the middle of the cylinder kept it spinning. Once a Tibetan symbol of faith, these prayer mills were becoming increasingly rare, and the paintings of gods on rocks were fading. But the mumbling continued. Most Tibetans are indifferent to the rise in living standards brought about by China's rule. Spiritual life is dying out, and they have nothing to counter this with except their mumbling.

On my second morning in Lhasa I met up with Tashi, a young Tibetan exile who had just returned from Katmandu. He was to trek with me for a couple of weeks into the mountains and be my bearer and interpreter. I gave him equipment and promised to pay him in dollars at the end of the trip. But what interested him most was visiting the wild regions of Tibet and traveling the roads over which, in 1959, his relatives had been carted off to concentration camps in the north. Many had been shipped from Lhasa to the Tengger Shamo Desert, an extension of the Gobi Desert. The Chi-

nese had come to the monasteries of the Lhasa valley and surrounding areas with long convoys of trucks to round up the monks,
many of them only teenagers. The journey subjected them to dust
and icy wind as they crossed mountain passes over sixteen thousand
feet high. Nighttime brought no respite either. Prisoners were
herded into tiny holding pens outside the villages and forced to
stand all night.

Tashi, myself, and our driver, a man named Sonam, traveled this
very same road north in a rented Toyota until we reached Nachu,
where we spent the night with Amdo people. I found a place to lie
down—among dogs and a dozen or so Tibetans—but I could not
fall asleep. The snoring, the fleas, the smoke, not to mention my fear
that we wouldn't find enough gas to continue our journey, kept me
awake. On top of everything else, there was traffic all night on the
nearby road. Rockets capable of reaching northern India were sta-
tioned near this town, which lay two hundred miles northeast of
Lhasa. These medium-range rockets were transported on ten-axled
vehicles and were now part of the new Tibet—along with hundreds
of thousands of Chinese soldiers.

The following day Sonam took Tashi and me to the military
base on the border between Amdo and Kham. This was strictly forbidden, and we made sure to stay out of sight. Sonam drove back to
Lhasa alone, leaving Tashi and me to figure out which way to go. We
planned to walk all the way to Alando in eastern Tibet, though neither of us knew the old caravan trails. We walked for ten miles
through the darkness, returning to where we had spent the previous
night, and managed to avoid the police.

I asked Tashi to get some beer in the village and was sound
asleep when two policemen appeared and asked me for my passport.

"I don't understand," I told them.

"Passport!" one of them shouted.

"I came here by bus from Lhasa, and tomorrow I'm going back
to Lhasa by bus."

Now they were the ones who couldn't understand me.

I knew full well that they wanted my passport, even if only to detain me. When Tashi returned, a bottle of beer in each hand, they threatened to arrest us if I didn't produce a passport. Tashi caught on right away and played along. He explained that we were planing to return to Lhasa the following day.

"No! We are taking you to Nachu tomorrow!" one of the policemen yelled (Tashi translating). They left at midnight, after Tashi promised that we would wait for them to come for us the next morning.

An hour later we stole out of the village without using our flash-lights. We hid under a tree for about an hour and then set off for Nachu, keeping a safe distance from the gravel road.

Shortly before dawn we emerged from a narrow gorge and came upon fields lying alongside a river. The road was far above us, like a faint brushstroke, and above it, perched on a rock, was a small Tibetan village, gray cubes piled up on each other against the black rock face.

We scrambled up the embankment and reached the road, our legs buckling under the weight of our backpacks. Looking left and right, we crossed the road and continued climbing the slope toward the village. Suddenly I staggered and heard the sound of crashing waves in my ears. Tottering, I came to a stop. My heart was racing. I heard a gurgling sound in my throat, a sound that I imagined must precede death by asphyxiation. I stood there, bent over and gasping for air, then turned to look at Tashi, who was lying facedown. It looked as if he were writhing in pain. Our scramble up the hillside in the thin air of this altitude had nearly killed us.

Once our hearts and lungs had recovered a little, we continued up the path along the cracked walls of houses until we came to a small hut next to a waterfall. Bluish spirals of smoke rose over the tiled roof and were blown down into the valley by the cold wind coming down off the mountain.

Day was fast breaking, but we were too far from the road to worry about being spotted by the police. We asked the inhabitants of the hut for some yogurt, which they kindly provided. We ate our breakfast and continued up the mountainside. Only Tibetans lived in these remote valleys, so we no longer worried about being detected. The power of the Chinese government extended only to where the roads went. Nomads living beneath the Nakula, a snow-covered pass, let us sleep in a stable next to their goats. I asked them while they were milking the goats—as off-handedly as I could, with Tashi's help—whether any chemos were in these parts.

"No," they all answered.

"How about in Nachu?"

"None there either."

"And in Shigatse?"

"No."

"In Lhasa?"

They laughed.

"Yes," one of them said. "There used to be one in the Norbu-linka zoo."

"Where else can they be found?"

"Maybe behind Nakula, in Takung, and farther down."

We were on the right track.

Two days later, through fog and fresh snow, we crossed Nakula. In the evening we came upon two nomad tents and were invited in to spend the night. The goats had just been herded up; yaks stood around the tents in the hollow of the valley, snow speckling their black fur.

The simple family tent, made of yak hair, was barely sixteen feet square and had a wide slit in its hatch for ventilation. It was intricately constructed and yet resilient. The outside was decorated with strips of cloth and held up by nearly thirty drawstrings made of yak hair. The poles and stakes were of wood, thick as arms. Ghost traps and scarecrows were set up nearby to protect the animals, and a large black guard dog was chained to a wooden stake. Prayer flags fluttered above a small altar on which juniper, dried fruit, and *tsampa* were burnt in sacrifice every morning.

The tent was tightly packed. To the right of the entrance were sacks of pressed cheese, a container of cooked meat, a trunk filled with supplies, and a few yak-hide sacks of barley. To the left were water containers—two made of wood and one of clay—a cask of butter, a pail of milk, a bucket of yogurt, and a basket filled with cheeses. In the middle of the tent were yet more trunks on which sat two large millstones. Behind the trunks stood an oven covered with pots and kitchen utensils, such as scrapers, knives, spoons, and pot-cleaners. Next to them were extra food containers with dried cream, as well as a *tsampa* sack and pats of yak dung. There was also a special oven for roasting barley. Behind all that was the family altar on which sat bowls of holy water, butter lamps, and a treasure chest. On a little table beside the altar were two drinking bowls, two *tsampa* bowls, and two prayer wheels. To the left were sacks containing what I imagined to be the family fortune, which could be added to but not taken from.

The tent faced the mountain, and in front of it lay heaps of yak dung piled up into a little wall to dry. These dung pats are used both as fuel and as a buffer against the wind. There was no animal pen, but the goats and the ewes with their calves were tied in a tight circle surrounded by yak calves. Surrounding the calves were the full-grown yaks and cows.

There was a reason for this system. Chemos, they said, roamed at night in search of food through the vast regions between the uppermost villages and the glaciers. The villagers arranged their animals so as to protect the smaller and younger ones.

At these altitudes there were few forests, but there were bears and quite a few wolves. The tree line lay at about thirteen thousand feet; barley can grow at altitudes of up to fourteen thousand feet. During the summer months, the yak herds climb ever higher up the mountain slopes, up to eighteen thousand feet. The glaciers begin at eighteen thousand to nineteen thousand feet. In these remote parts between glacial mountains, the Tibetans speak of the chemo as if discussing an everyday animal. This marauder shuns paths trod by humans and makes large circles around tents and settlements, but has stolen meat. Even though he shies from all contact with humans, he sometimes manages to kill and drag off a yak or a goat, either alone or with others of his kind.

"Chemos are not only strong, they are also very cunning," I heard the women say as Tashi and I prepared our beds for the night.

The rare encounters between humans and chemos have not only inspired fear in the local people, but led to their belief that chemos are intelligent predators. You can't catch one with traps, bush-beating, or religious spells.

When the men entered the tent later, swords at their sides, they set one of the little tables with *tsampa* bowls, sliced some dried meat, and invited us to join them. The teapot stood on the stove, along with five other pots that were alternately placed over the second fire-hole. One woman sat weaving at a loom; another was busy grinding *tsampa*. Everything was done deliberately, and we never got the feeling that we were intruding.

In eastern Tibet the nomads wear simple pelt coats and no complicated head ornaments. The only thing reminiscent of their past riches is their jewelry—amber, turquoise, and corals in their hair, and chi stones worn on a string around their necks.

I hesitantly asked if anyone in the tent had ever seen a chemo. Everyone pointed at the woman at the loom, who looked at me.

"What did he look like?" I asked Tashi to ask her.

"Big and thickset."

"Like a human?"

"Yes, as big as a human, but heavier and with big feet. Long hair everywhere. On his head, too."

"What color skin did he have?"

"His face and palms were black, his flat nose, too. Big nostrils."

"His mouth?"

"Wide, with hair all round."

"What about his teeth?"

"Much bigger than a man's."

"And his eyes?"

"I was frightened by the yellow of his eyes."

We stared at the woman. It suddenly felt as if we were huddling closer together in the tent. The nocturnal valley outside had taken on an uncanny aura.

The following day I saw some faint footprints on the edge of the trail to Tshagu. They were about a foot long and eight inches wide. The space between each print was roughly the length of my own stride.

In the following weeks I came near these mysterious animals twice. Once was at dusk, when two creatures suddenly appeared, high up by the edge of the forest. They crouched down for an instant, then quickly rushed back into the forest as I took a snapshot of them. One click of the shutter and they were gone. I thought they might be bears, but I couldn't be sure if they were brown bears or Himalayan black bears.

I spent whole nights trailing chemos with a local man, and on one occasion, in a field of young barley plants between a village and the forest, we heard a whistle. We found footprints and tracked them night after night in the rain.

Just before ten one night, I was lying in wait again in the pouring rain when suddenly two monstrous figures loomed out of the darkness against the clouds and the forest. I pressed the shutter release of my Leica, but the flash failed, and the creatures ran away into the darkness.

By now I was certain that the yeti had to be a chemo. What I needed was photographic proof.

7

CURIOSITY AND RIDICULE

Trekking back to Lhasa was like running a gauntlet. The police had put up barriers on all the roads around Nachu shortly after our disappearance, and they were still checking everyone who passed. When we finally reached Lhasa, I asked Tashi not to tell anyone about our yeti expedition, and if possible to stay inside his house in Parkor. For a few more days I secretly went into town, going to stores and avoiding police checkpoints, then taking cabs back to the hotel in the evenings. I met four climbers, American and English, who had just made the first successful ascent up Mount Everest's feared eastern wall. They looked awful. Their faces had been ravaged by sun and frost, their lips were cracked, and their hands were bandaged. They had been trapped on the wall for a number of days, unable to return to the base camp, without any food or enough to drink.

I saw them staggering along the sidewalk and called out to congratulate them, but they didn't react. All four seemed to be limping. One kept looking over in my direction and waving his arms in a strange way. I couldn't understand why.

Chris Bonington, Britain's most famous climber, was also in town. He spoke of seeing strange tracks and mentioned a pelt that his crew had found during an expedition to Menlungtse, on the border between Tibet and Nepal.

We talked late into the night. Ed Webster was there, as was Steve Venebels, both excellent climbers, and I had the feeling that they had experienced more on the Menlungtse or Mount Everest than they had come to grips with. Webster still seemed disoriented.

I held my interest in the yeti in check, since the others seemed not to have given this matter much thought. If we weren't on the same wavelength, we would have ended up talking past each other.

One day, I was in the middle of Parkor when suddenly plainclothes policemen carrying guns and radios went running past me. The Tibetans scattered in panic; an old woman next to me began crying, and a distraught cripple, who had been cringing by the roadside, dragged himself into the nearest doorway. A truck blocked the way of the fleeing crowds; tear gas was in the air. Six young lamas who had been carrying a banner proclaiming "Free Tibet!" were hauled into a truck, which raced off, sirens blaring. Columns of soldiers marched in; then came trucks and more soldiers, their clean olive-green uniforms clashing starkly with the Tibetans' dirty rags. Within half an hour the disturbance was over, and Parkor lay empty.

Tibet has always been rich in myths and legends, poor in freedom. Its history does not go back much further than the reign of King Srongtsen Gompo, who managed to unite the many tribes of the high plateaus in the seventh century A.D. This became the kingdom of Tufan, and Lhasa, "the City of the Sun," was its capital.

King Gompo set up Tibet's first ties with China by marrying Wen Cheng, a Chinese princess, as can still be seen depicted in the ancient frescoes on monastery walls. Gompo also married a Nepalese princess. This first king of Tibet was a pragmatic man. But Tibet never again quite managed to emancipate itself fully from China.

In the eleventh century, the balance of power in Tibet shifted again, this time because of religion. Lamaism was spreading, and Tibet became transformed into a monastic state. But the various religious communities continued to vie for power, and at the beginning of the fifteenth century a lama named Tsongkhapa intensified the struggle, and Lamaism split permanently into two factions.

Only in 1912, after the Chinese Manchu dynasty had fallen and England was trying to extend its influence from India to Lhasa, did the thirteenth Dalai Lama, deeply loved by his people, declare Tibet free from vassalage. For the next forty years China lost almost all its influence over Tibet.

When the Communist Party began rebuilding China's authority, and Chairman Mao ordered that the Tibetan people be "liberated" in 1950, Tibet's de facto independence was over. The Chinese Liberation Army sent thirty thousand battle-tried soldiers into Tibet from the north and the east. The small, weak Tibetan army didn't stand a chance. There were some mock negotiations, followed by military deployment.

By September 9, 1951, the Chinese aggressors had moved into the holy city. The Tibetans were humiliated and brutally suppressed. Monasteries were bombed, monks taunted, children abducted. The Chinese quickly seized political control of the country. When Panchen Lama criticized the inhuman conditions in the prisons, he was arrested and tortured. The conflict escalated, and the Dalai Lama fled the country in a dramatic escape in 1959. Many thousands of Tibetans followed him into exile in India, where he still lives today. The small kingdom of Nepal also granted asylum to thousands of Tibetans.

Ten thousand Tibetans were killed in Lhasa alone during the rebellion of March 10, 1959. The death toll in the whole country is said to have been as high as a hundred thousand. Thousands disappeared into prisons, many of them forever. Then, close on the heels of Tibet's "liberation" came the Cultural Revolution, which brought more "reeducation" and brutal subjugation. The Tibetans' long road of suffering was only beginning.

In 1965, Tibet was officially declared an autonomous province of China, but the repression continued, and though tourists were now permitted to travel there, Tibetan demonstrations during 1987 and 1988 set off a new era of repression. Freedom to travel within Tibet was again curbed.

Although the yeti myth had spread throughout the world, the creature's actual existence, in which I now believed firmly, could only be established by going to where it lived. But as a foreigner, I could no longer travel to Tibet. The window had closed.

In the meantime, a new kind of yeti hysteria was sprouting in the West. Some scientists began to speculate that it might be possible that a few specimens of *Gigantopithecus*—presumed to have become extinct some three hundred thousand years ago—may have survived in Central Asia. A few zoologists supported this theory. Soon these gigantic apes were populating the imaginations of millions. As to the question of why nobody had ever found any, a simple answer was formulated: because these animals were shy and lived in remote areas. This somehow managed to ignore the fact that the four corners of the earth had been fully explored and observed by satellites.

The tale of the monster of the Virunga Mountains in Africa—who also had a penchant, it was said, for abducting women—had also at one time sounded completely implausible. John Speke, who discovered the source of the Nile, heard about them from King Rumanika of central Africa. When Oskar von Beringe wrote in 1902 that these "ape monsters that abducted the native women and, in passionate lust, crushed them to death" really existed, nobody would have believed him—had he not shot one.

Today we know almost all there is to know about the gorillas of the mountains of Rwanda. During the twentieth century these mountain creatures have been transformed in our minds from monsters to gentle giants. Could the same thing not happen with the yeti? I wondered. Did I have to shoot one to convince skeptics that the abominable snowman was in fact nothing more than a peaceful animal?

One explorer wrote me to say that anthropoids were still living in Africa today. As with the yeti, only gigantic footprints had been found. I declined the invitation to join in the search.

Every week something about the yeti appeared in the newspapers, and every day I received letters full of questions and "helpful" information. Most wanted to know where I was hoping to encounter my next yeti, and when I was intending to furnish proof of its existence. When I decided to let only tradition and a few Himalayan farmers guide me, a new road opened up before me.

In October 1988, Hamburg's Thalia Theater staged a play called *Yeti—the Wild Man,* by Gao Xingjian. The main idea was not to portray reality, but to explore new ways of imagining nature. The playwright and his director, Lin Zhaohua, wanted to show how civilization was destroying the natural world, and they did this by dramatizing different encounters between Chinese farmers and so-called wild men. Here is an example.

On June 6, 1977, in the province of Shaanxi, a man named Pang Gensheng was mowing his lawn when he suddenly realized a "hairy man" was standing right in front of him. They were eyeball to eyeball. This is how Pang's encounter is described:

He was about seven and a half feet tall, with wide shoulders and long arms, large hands, and a stride measuring five feet.

Pang threw a stone at the creature, injuring it, and it quickly fled. A few weeks later a second man, Yang Wanchun, claims to have seen the same "hairy man" in exactly the same place. Although the yeti must have noticed him, it came as close as seven or eight feet from Wanchun. A ditch was all that separated them. "As we stood opposite each other, the hairy human made eleven or twelve different sounds: the chirping of a sparrow, the barking of a dog, the neighing of a pony, the growling of a leopard, the crying of an infant. He made these sounds incessantly for over an hour. Finally I took a few steps back, picked up a rock, and threw it at the hairy human, hitting him in the chest. He yelled and ran off, howling, in a southeasterly direction. He climbed up the side of a hill pretty quickly, holding on to trees and branches. . . . His feet were like those of a human, wide in front and narrow at the back, but they were well over a foot long. You could tell from the prints in the muddy earth that his toenails were pretty long, and that his five toes were clearly separated from one another. It was obviously a male animal. It was definitely not a black bear, a golden ape, or a giant panda!

One detail in Yang Wanchun's description made me a little suspicious—the clear imprint of the creature's toenails—but during the performance I quickly forgot this detail, and, for two hours, my yeti. The protagonist in Gao Xingjian's story is an ecologist who sets off into the wilderness to study animals on the brink of extinction. He keeps bumping into explorers from all over the world seeking the abominable snowman. This confrontation between the old world and the new reflects both man's need to reshape the world and to create the "wild man" myth. The result: modern man might ask as many questions as he can concerning the origin of the yeti, but he will not find the answers through scientific investigation alone. It is modern man who is the "wild man."

Unprepared to go to the Himalayas to seek answers, yeti buffs felt free to speculate that yetis might be living deep in the earth in caves near the north pole, or in "yeti clubs," which sounds like a sort of retirement community.

I knew I would learn nothing from the modern conception of the "wild man." A "yetic" language course was being offered at the Göttinger Adult Education Center: "No prior knowledge necessary." Those interested could study "the language of the mysterious Snowmen of the Himalayan highlands." Appropriately, the introductory class was to be held on April 1.

Another practical joke involved a yeti found in 1968 in a freezer in Minnesota. It was, said reports, a humanlike corpse covered with hair, supposedly discovered in rural Minnesota, in the trailer of an actor by the name of Hansen. The corpse was displayed in an enormous block of ice. Hansen claimed it came from Asia. Russian seal hunters had found it floating in the Bering Sea. After a wild odyssey, the corpse somehow ended up in the actor's trailer—nobody knows how. Zoologists drew pictures of this iceman and described his features as being those of a hominid. No one thought to crack the ice and remove tissue samples. And then one day the corpse simply disappeared. Unbelievers asserted it had been made of latex.

A far more compelling mystery was why half-man, half-animal creatures populated the imaginations of the shepherds, nomads, and farmers in the vast mountainous regions from Siberia to Mongolia, Tien Tshan to the Caucasus. They were simply a part of the fauna of their wilderness. And yet, since time immemorial, the people of those regions—like those gaping at the corpse of the Minnesota iceman—were convinced that these creatures were primitive men in a state of arrested development between ape and man. In the 1950s, a Russian yeti commission surveyed the indigenous peoples of the area and concluded in a report that the creatures they heard described were Neanderthals who had escaped extinction. This mixture of caveman, forest-man, and animal-man was fantasy. Yet it was also more than that. As long as the Himalayan inhabitants were convinced that these creatures had survived, and as long as we searched for them in the remotest mountain forests, the yeti did exist.

It was never my goal to shoot or capture a yeti and drag it into our world. It would quickly have turned into a mere object of curiosity, pitilessly studied under the microscope of science in the sterility of Western laboratories. There the myth would have died, victim to the same species that had initially created it. As long as we sought an early form of the human species and dreamt of a lost world that predated human history, we felt compelled to prove that the yeti existed.

For two years my search for the yeti was interrupted while I set out on a walk across Antarctica, a hostile environment in which I myself was the "snowman." Then in 1990, at an auction in England, quite by chance, I came across a sixteenth-century *tanka* on which two strange-looking animals were portrayed. Both stood upright. One was small, red-haired, and apelike, the other large and black, corresponding to the animal I had seen. I bought the tanka so that I could look at it at home, as if I could bring these painted animals back to life. Thus my research into the yeti continued.

My next yeti expedition took place in the spring of 1991. With the German television host Tina Radke, cameraman Fulvio Mariani, and photographer Paul Hanny, I set out to cross the length of the Kingdom of Bhutan. We trekked for weeks through the Himalayas, climbing to the highest pastures between Tibet and Bhutan, in search of tracks and tales in the regions below the glacial mountains and above the impenetrable forests. The climate, terrain, and vegetation created an ideal habitat for the yeti described in the legends.

Fortune seemed to smile on May 12, a cool and sunny day, in a lama monastery near the main road from Mendegang to Tongsa. We had gotten off to an early start. Just past the village of Wangoli, where there was a street market, we stopped to rest at Gangtey Gompa, a small monastery. The monks in the courtyard did not seem to mind our sitting down among them. There wasn't the slightest hint of a breeze, and the sun beat down on the worn flagstones on which we sat. The facade of the monastery and the solitary, glowing clouds above made it feel as if the silence around us could elevate anything terrestrial into the endless cosmos. Only the oxblood-colored strip beneath the roof of straw, wood, and woven twigs gave the monastery the look of an earthly structure.

We asked if we would be allowed to enter the *gompa,* the main meditation chamber. The monks responded by leading us up a steep exterior wooden staircase. With lively gestures, they motioned us to come up to the second floor.

Once in the *gompa* I peered out narrow, barred windows at the wide, hilly land. Sunlight was filtering through the small windows barely the width of a hand into the narrow passages and prayer rooms through which we walked. I scrutinized the sooty walls for paintings. There were no yeti pictures. I asked if there was a tantric chamber and was told that it was locked and that strangers were not permitted entrance.

I pulled some paper money out of my pocket. "A contribution for your monastery," I said. A young lama in wine-red robes brought a key, and the door to the tantric chamber was opened.

We crowded in. A single golden shimmer seeped through the narrow window of the tiny, wood-paneled room. My eyes slowly grew accustomed to the gloom and I looked around. On the walls masks hung alongside skulls painted on cloth. Above them were stuffed animal heads, like hunting trophies, of elk, bear, wild boar, sheep, and deer. And nailed to the wall by the back of its scalp was the hide of a "red yeti," as the lama told us. I was trembling with excitement. Bones were still attached to the relic's hands and legs, and on its head, which was largely bald, hung a long black hank of hair.

A flash went off.

"No photographs!" hissed one of the older lamas who had come in after us, gesturing that we had been shown enough. We were allowed to film nothing. Even had we been allowed to, the photos might have been dark. I touched the yeti pelt and bones. I would have given anything for a few seconds of sunlight.

With shameless curiosity I asked our hosts what this object was.

"The head and hide of a yeti cub," the oldest monk replied quietly. "Four hundred years ago, the *ringpoche* of the monastery put a spell on the evil creature with his magical powers, killed it, and had it brought here."

"Why is the hide all that is left?"

"Everything else was removed: its heart, its bones. Only its head, feet, and hands remain."

I sniffed the scalp and looked at it more closely. Again a flash went off, and for an instant I could see better. The few hairs on the scalp had clearly been stuck in, and little sticks and threads supported the fingers and toes.

Outside, in the courtyard of the monastery, I felt frustration and disappointment. I knew the mummy was fake.

The barley stood knee-high in the wide valleys beneath the monastery, but few people were in the fields. The farmers here are the descendants of Tibetan nomads, whose religion, Lamaism, is threaded through with tantric images. Their beliefs, like shamanism, unified all of nature—water, earth, wind, clouds, fire, and love—with the divine. Perhaps the yeti is simply part of their animistic view of the world. Perhaps I would find no concrete evidence of the *mygio*.

Mighty coniferous trees stood before the walls of the monastery, and the stillness was interrupted only by the barking dogs fighting over the leftover scraps of our meal, which they dragged to the edge of a meadow to devour.

I decided to go back into the gloomy tantric chamber to confirm my suspicions. The hands and legs really did seem human, like those of a child of eight or nine. It was obvious they were shaped with little sticks, leather, cloth, and thread—in other words, re-created. They were hanging on a thin hide that looked as if it might have been that of a monkey. They head was clearly handcrafted, its face a mask, and the hide stretched over it probably that of an animal. I couldn't tell if what was beneath it was wood or bone.

The only truly meaningful thing was its position on the wall. Hanging below it in the tantric chamber were the heads of elk, wild boars, tigers, black bears, and sheep. Thus the *mygio* was ranked above animals. The lamas confirmed this. The elder stressed that their *mygio* corresponded to a *dremo* cub from Tibet.

The Gangtey Gompa relic was nothing more than a doll used to cast out spirits—or to keep the legend of the yeti alive. But why would these lamas, who were educated men, want to perpetuate a myth that might well be of shamanistic provenance and no longer fit their conception of the world? Could the yeti simply be an invention of the lamas, a symbol of the antihuman that they wanted to cultivate in the imagination of the people?

I no longer knew what to think. Only one thing was clear to me: the yeti did not fit into a rational, tangible world and could only have originated here, either as a product of the imagination, or as an emblem of some rare animal.

We drove to the east of Bhutan through forests and ravines and over passes with countless sharp bends. It rained constantly. Fog hugged the mountain flanks. Waterfalls cascaded down onto the roads. When we could no longer continue by Jeep, we loaded our belongings onto a dozen horses and continued on foot.

In the north we were told that a few years back, near Laya, a yeti had abducted a woman. The king of Bhutan had immediately ordered gamekeepers, shepherds, and soldiers with radios and guns to comb the mountains. Any sightings were to be immediately radioed to the palace in Thimphu. But there were no encounters with yetis, nor even any tracks. The king finally called off the search. The woman reappeared months later.

We trekked almost 350 miles, braving snakes, wild boars, and leeches. We were convinced that one morning we would see a figure in the fog—appearing from the underbrush or cedar forest or perhaps stepping out from between two rocks. He would remain in our field of vision long enough for us to take a picture: an abominable snowman frozen in time. All the work of the past five years would in one instant be vindicated. I would hand the pictures around to my skeptics and say, "Here he is!" And yet—and yet—all I would have was a picture, nothing more than a picture.

The path coiled up the mountain and we followed it for days on end, losing all sense of direction. Only when we started heading down a mountain slope did the clouds open up. People working in the pastures by the edge of the woods told us where we were and where we could set up camp.

We adapted to life with the nomads and their sheep and yaks—we drank buttermilk in the evenings, ate dried yak meat for lunch, passed smoky evenings in conversation. When storms began brewing, we fled into their tents.

Once, in a clearing in the woods we came across a herd of fifty or so wild boars. They tore off in a wild stampede, and our porters, many of them barefoot, raced after them. It was many hours before we could continue our trek.

We sighted neither a black yeti nor a red one, but an aged man told us, covering his mouth with his hand, that he had seen a yeti eleven years ago below Laya.

"Were you alone?" we asked him.

"Yes, I was alone. He was alone, too. It was a foggy evening."

"What did this animal look like?"

"He stood upright in front of me, over seven feet tall, totally covered with hair. A tousled mop of hair covered his face."

The man had the facial features of a Tibetan, and when he spoke of his encounter, it was as if he was ridding himself of a great burden. He may not have told anyone else of this encounter from fear of bringing a curse upon himself.

Misfortune did befall his family, he lamented. A few days after his encounter, his father died without any warning. Belief that the yeti brought misfortune was why it was so difficult to get details from the local population.

But we did not give up. Everywhere we went I asked the farmers and the nomads if they had seen any yetis.

One member of our group, Paul, fell ill from dysentery. A red line went from his ankle all the way up to his lymph nodes—a sign of blood poisoning, probably from leeches. Paul was usually so energetic and curious, his camera always at the ready, but now he simply sat unresponsively on a mule. He became so weak and lost so much weight that within a few days we had to radio for a helicopter to pick him up. He took with him the film of the red yeti relic we had been shown at the Gangtey Gompa. He was both proud of this picture and afraid that he had brought a curse upon himself and would soon die.

We all breathed a sigh of relief when we heard the helicopter that was to fly him to India. It rose up from the rain-heavy fog below us in the valley.

"The yeti isn't an abominable snowman, right?" Paul asked me.

"No," I said, patting him on the shoulder. "And he isn't a harbinger of misfortune either."

Laya, a village famous for its view of two snow-covered mountains, consists of a hundred houses and five thousand yaks. The inhabitants originally came from Tibet, like the Sherpas; one valley and a mountain crest comprise their entire world. It is only a four-day trek to Gyangtse in Tibet, and people in Laya talked of the *dremo* and the *tshute* as if sightings were daily occurrences. Yeti tales are told along with yak tales as though there were no difference between mythical time and the present.

Every evening I went looking for yeti tracks, but all I saw was a takin, a rare animal—an antelope-like goat—about which the mountain dwellers tell the following tale:

One day an old farmer went to a wise man and asked for his help.

"You are wise and knowledgeable, and well versed in

magic," the old farmer said. He then placed all kinds of bones on the table in front of the wise man: the nasal bone of a horse, the skull of an elk, the horns of a mountain goat, the thighbones of a yak.

"Make an animal for me from these bones," the old farmer begged him.

"Why not," the wise man said. And the animal that he made was a takin.

The yeti belongs in a different category from the takin, which has been conclusively classified, but both are a combination of animal and legend. Here, where everything has its corresponding half—yin and yang—the yeti, too, is understood as a double creature. And both halves are still alive: the mythological and the real.

Only Laya's town drunk was prepared to tell anyone who would listen about his encounter with the yeti, while steadily pouring *tshang* down his throat. Babbling on with sweeping gestures, he listened neither to the entreaties of my porters nor to the admonishments of his fellow villagers. Chortling, he told of "forest people" who broke the spines of the sheep and then dragged shepherd girls off to their caves. He knew victims of these monsters, or at least professed to know them. When I asked him if he knew anything definite about dremos, chemos, or yetis, he spat *tshang* into the fire. "Me!" he shouted. *"I'm a yeti!"*

Our journey ended with a trek from Changotang to Paro. I saw a large Himalayan black bear, called *ladom* in this region, but no yeti.

With every journey to Tibet, I moved further and further away from the popular concept of the yeti. And with every year the scorn of the yetologists grew.

People sent me caricatures. There were jokes about my being unable to capture the yeti on film. Questions about my abominable snowman were now inevitable at readings and conferences. My most severe critics were the ones who confused the yeti of their imagination with the real thing and would only accept as conclusive evidence photographs reflecting their vision of the yeti. But how could I fulfill their fantasies?

I continued my quest, ignoring the scientists who found me amusing and the fantasists for whom I unlocked secret aspirations. It wasn't my job to confirm or refute what millions imagined the yeti to be.

8

"GLACIAL COSMOGONY" AND
"ANCESTRAL LEGACY"

S hortly after a documentary on our journey through Bhutan
was aired on German television in late 1991, I received a letter
from a Mr. Schäfer. This letter contained some facts about the yeti
that I found informative:

In 1934, General Liu Hsiang, the former warlord of the province
of Sichuan, had asked me to uncover the mystery of the yeti and
to bring him a male and female pair of these longhaired "Snowmen" for his zoo. The following year I had the opportunity to
set out on such an expedition to the uninhabitable regions of
Inner Tibet, to the source of the Yangtze River. There I shot a
number of yetis, in the form of the mighty Tibetan bear.

In 1933–35, the British mountaineers Frank Smythe and
Eric Shipton discovered the first "yeti footprints," and pub-

lished the pictures they took in *The London Illustrated News* and in *Paris Match*. This created a sensation. The "Abominable Snowman" aroused the interest of journalists and opened up financial resources for numerous Everest expeditions. In 1938, after I had uncovered the whole sham in my publications with Senckenberg in Frankfurt and established the yeti's real identity with the pictures and pelts of my Tibetan bears, Smythe and Shipton came to me on their knees, begging me not to publish my findings in the English-speaking press. The secret had to be kept at all costs—"Or else the press won't give us the money we need for our next Everest expedition."

This Mr. Schäfer was doubtless the explorer and zoologist Ernst Schäfer, who had been chosen to head Operation Tibet, a secret 1939 mission sponsored by the German Reich. The Schäfer Unit's assignment was to "incite the Tibetan army against the British troops." The mission never took place, however, and the Schäfer Unit was reassigned to Ancestral Legacy, a pseudoscientific department of the SS.

Before his work on "ancestral legacy," Schäfer had been an ornithologist of international renown. He had also become an expert in zoology, botany, agriculture, and ethnology, and was one of the foremost Tibetan specialists of his time. "This mightiest of the earth's high plateaus is a land of wonder, variety, and surprise, which time and again casts a spell over the lone explorer," he wrote in the preface to his book *Dach der Erde* (The Roof of the World), published in Berlin in 1938. "It is an immense, sequestered space, many times the size of the German Reich, hemmed in to the south by the giant mountain ranges of the Himalayas, to the east by the Hsifan highlands, to the north by the armor-plated giant peaks of the Kunlun Mountains, and to the west by the Pamirs."

I wondered whether Schäfer knew more about the yeti than he was letting on, so I wrote him a letter: "As we seem to have similar theories concerning the yeti, and I am of the opinion that most people have the wrong image of this 'being,' I would be grateful if you could answer a few questions," I wrote.

Shortly before he died on July 21, 1992, Schäfer wrote back, "The Tibetans call yetis *dremu*. In western China, they are also called *migiö*, and in the land of the Golden River, *beshung*, white bear, even though the *beshung*, or panda, don't exist in that region." The information about the panda was new to me; the rest I had confirmed. I disagreed with Schäfer's second assertion, however—that the reason yeti footprints do not correspond with bear paw prints is that the sun's rays melt the snow. After all, fresh tracks in the snow had often been sighted.

Schäfer also stated that every yeti sighting involved a "Tibetan brown bear with varying fur color."

All these bears belong to the same species of *ursus*, to which also the brown bear and the grizzly bear belong. Early explorers, from Britain as well as from Russia, made the mistake of assuming that the color variations of the Tibetan bear pointed to different species. I managed to resolve this problem through my research (published by Senckenbergische Naturforschende Gesellschaft, Frankfurt/Main, 1936). Tibetan black bears belong to another family of bears and are found all the way from the Himalayas to the Ussuri basin.

Schäfer had done his research in eastern Tibet, the same region where I had made my own discoveries in 1986 and 1988. "I shot most of my yetis," he wrote, "near the sources of the Mekong, the Yangtze, and the Hwang Ho, but mainly in the completely uninhabited Kunlun Mountains. Current informants who have visited these areas in the last few decades, however, either by Jeep or by flying over them, reported that they did not spot any black bears. Tibetan nomads nowadays are often armed with automatic rifles, which might well explain things."

I read through Ernst Schäfer's books on Tibet, and although he provides a wealth of interesting data about pandas and Tibetan bears, he does not present any clear proof that one of them corresponds to the yeti. Schäfer had observed the *beshung,* or white bear, which we know as the giant panda *(Ailuropola melanoleuca).* At the time, its classification had been "very controversial, and little was known about its geographical distribution or its behavior patterns." He had observed that the panda "was a querulous loner," and that the Tibetan black bear had become "a real scourge in these parts":

> The Tibetan black bear is large with an exceptionally fleshy build and powerful paws that are covered with thick fur all the way down to the soles of its feet. Its fur is dense, beautiful, and jet-black, and around the bear's neck is a distinctive ruff of long, relatively soft hair. One of its salient characteristics is a broad white strip that runs along the base of its neck in a crescent encircling the region of its collarbone. This "ring" can vary greatly in form and size. Depending on the geographical region, its coloring can vary from white to yellow, or a yellowish gold.
>
> The distribution of this animal, which has been incorrectly named *Selenarctos tibetanus* (since it does not inhabit the steppes of Inner Tibet), ranges east from the high Himalayas, reaching across the Sino-Tibetan border provinces of Yunnan and Sichuan along the edge of the high mountain ranges, all the way north to Korea.

Dach der Erde, which enjoyed great success in Germany in the early 1940s, contained accounts about the yeti that came close to my own findings:

> One morning, a Wata came to me with a fantastic tale about a Snowman roaming around in the high mountains. He is as big as a yak, hairy as a bear, and walks on two legs like a man, and the soles of his feet are supposedly reversed, so that no

one can follow his tracks. He is a night creature, descending deep into the valleys, wreaking havoc with the natives' herds, tearing humans to pieces and then dragging them up the mountain to his terrain near the glaciers.

Schäfer offered a reward to anyone who could lead him to the den of this snowman and tried to convince his guides that it was just an ordinary bear. The Wata who had initially told Schäfer about the gigantic footprints in the snow urged him to give up the hunt. The Wata had been looking for some animals that had strayed from his herd and had seen the snowman's head emerging from a cave. It was an enormous head, covered with long, whitish hair, and was as frightening as a monster's.

Something was in the cave when Schäfer got there, something yellowish in the gloomy twilight. Before he could determine whether this was the head or the rump of the thing, he was stunned by an overwhelming stench. He backed away and, standing about seven or eight feet away from the mouth of the cave, threw some stones into it. Suddenly a mighty head appeared—no flying sparks, no flashing fangs. Schäfer aimed his rifle and pulled the trigger. The bear fell dead to the ground.

Schäfer knew there was nothing heroic about "shooting a bear that had just woken from its sleep with a modern automatic rifle at a range of eight feet," but he saw it as his "task as a zoologist to shed light, once and for all, on the unresolved matter of these bears."

These Tibetan bears differ from brown bears and grizzly bears through their thick, longhaired fur, and a cranium that is strongly developed in relation to their body. The Tibetan bears that have been classified to date are the Isabelle bear *(Ursus isabellinus)* from western Tibet, the mighty Tibetan blue bear *(Ursus pruinosus),* which has a longhaired, bluish-black fur with silver speckles and is from northern Tibet, and the regular Tibetan bear *(Ursus lagomyiarius)* from northeastern Tibet. Of these three types, very few specimens have been studied, and as a result accurate zoological classification has been impossible. I later managed to prove conclusively that earlier zoologists, who had never conducted research in situ, had been misled by age and gender variations into believing they were looking at different types of Tibetan bears. Young bears up to the age of three or four years have very light fur that can range in color from ocher-brown to a clear white. They correspond to the description of the Isabelle bear. Older female bears and mature male bears have darker, grizzly fur, with patches around the nape and shoulder areas ranging from a clear white to a yellowish gold. These bears correspond to the older (and very precise) Russian descriptions of the Tibetan bear *(Ursus lagomyiarius)*. Only the old dominant males are very dark in color and correspond to the "blue bears."

How Schäfer managed to classify the "snowman" as a bear before he had even seen one was a mystery to me. Even more inexplicable was why the natives first spoke of a "snowman roaming around in the high mountains," but then quickly changed their minds when Schäfer told them that this snowman was just "an ordinary bear, a *mashiung,* maybe—a large one!" If we are to believe Schäfer, the natives were suddenly convinced beyond all doubt that this creature was a large bear. Moreover, the fact that the natives "were so frightened of this bear that they not only avoided it at all costs, but pronounced its name with surprising veneration," contradicts his previous assertion. Furthermore, Schäfer continuously stresses the "ferocity and bloodthirstiness of the terrifying *dre-mu,* the 'devil's grandmother,' as the natives call this bear."

Time and again Schäfer describes how one of these *dremu* would rise threateningly on its hind legs: "When upright, it assumes a wild, almost human stance. With a deep growl it roars three times, quickly turns, and flees up the slope, only to stop suddenly dead in its tracks." He also describes the *chemo* as "massive, powerful, and mighty, a primal, wild predator; when shot, it rises to its full superhuman stature, turns a few times growling, and then falls forward."

The zoologist in Schäfer enjoys observing the behavior of these large predators. He notes how they lift their powerful heads and test the wind, their ears raised. "What an impressive sight when one stands in the vicinity of one of these shaggy fellows—his face filled with curiosity and snorting anger." Here is Schäfer the hunter speaking, not Schäfer the zoologist.

Schäfer also managed to observe a female bear "with her three charming little cubs that were no larger than house cats":

> They followed her, playing and tumbling about. Looking at this mighty female bear with her tiny offspring, I find it hard to believe that these charming little balls of wool should be the children of this massive ogress. I have never before seen a bear whose every move and gesture was as premeditated as this bear mother's was. Every time she ripped a clump of grass out of the earth and flung it behind her with a powerful swing, she first sat awhile, looking at her cubs. The small brood seemed to feel perfectly safe under the watchful eye of their mother. The cubs bit each other, pummeled each other with their tiny paws, rolled around all over the place, and took little if any notice of their mother. When the three little sprites ventured too far, she would turn and growl at them, and the cubs—as if frightened that she would punish them—trotted behind her again for a few seconds in single file.

One day four animals, foraging for food, appeared right in front of Schäfer's caravan. "Growling, they stood on their hind legs like gigantic humans, eyeing us undecidedly, as if they wanted to block our way. But suddenly the dark dominant males moved toward us with raised heads, sucking in air, and I suddenly realized that the caravan behind me, rattling and clattering, was dispersing in panic into the marshy bogs."

But Schäfer's account does not provide all the answers. In 1960, he had already become "certain he had come close to answering the yeti question," but he had only given half the answer. It was clear he was less interested in solving the mystery than in ridding the natives of their "disastrous superstition that the demons would kill us to a man because we had infuriated the local spirits by killing the bears." In order to "finally put an end to these hair-raising suppositions, these pestilent superstitions," he gave his porters "a scientific lecture on the origin of snowstorms." He wanted his porters to believe "that the will of a white man was more powerful than all the mountain spirits whirling about in their heads." The "devilish evil" that Schäfer claims to have seen in the Tibetan chemos, "their shifty nature," seems to have been inspired from quite a different superstition, from the hubris of the "master race."

In the 1930s, the yeti was of no further interest either to Schäfer the scientist or Schäfer the hunter. And what seemed to have been more important to him twenty years later was covering up the period of his life after his three Tibet expeditions, when he worked for the SS and Ancestral Legacy. Not until 1960 did he describe the highlands of central Tibet as "an area uninhabited for thousands of miles, but where according to the natives' beliefs the Snowman is the uncontested ruler." What snowman? The Tibetan bear? The dremos, chemos, or beshungs exist as yetis only insofar as one believes in their mythical existence. And this is why Schäfer's 1960 equation, that snowman equals yeti equals Tibetan bear, is incorrect.

The matter is far more complex and contradictory than Schäfer allows. His zoological work is legitimate enough, but after his work for Ancestral Legacy his reputation as a scientist was compromised. The aim of Ancestral Legacy was "to study the area, spirit, deeds, and legacy of the northern Indo-Germanic race." Schäfer had taken part in the first Tibetan expedition of the American scientist

Brooke Dolan from 1930 to 1932. He went on a second Tibetan expedition with Dolan in 1936. On his return to Germany, he was made an SS officer and joined Himmler's personal staff. He was not a man to dabble in esoteric matters.

In April 1938, Schäfer planned his own scientific expedition—SS Expedition Schäfer—to Tibet. Himmler, however, also wanted the expedition to explore prehistoric and linguistic issues. Locating the "core of the Nordic-Aryan legacy" was of paramount importance to him.

In 1939, Schäfer took on Himmler's special mission, the details of which remain unclear to this day. The idea was that, with the help of Germany's new ally, the Soviet Union, Schäfer would turn himself into a German "Lawrence of the Himalayas," and with a unit of thirty men incite Afghans and Tibetans against the British, destabilizing their hold on India. The project was cancelled in 1940 through Hitler's personal intervention.

In January 1940, Schäfer became the head of the Ancestral Legacy Division for Central Asian Studies and Expeditions. Dr. Bruno Beger was named as his associate. Beger was later put in charge of the racial analysis conducted by the Ancestral Legacy Division. A student of anthropology, he had taken part in Schäfer's 1938–39 Tibet expedition and had subsequently been excused from active military duty because of his "ongoing evaluation of the Tibetan material."

In August 1942, Schäfer was put in charge of a special expedition to the Caucasus. Beger was again to be his second-in-command. The project was called off in February 1943, and Schäfer's unit was elevated to the rank of Reich Institute and given the code name Sven Hedin, after the famous Swedish explorer. Schloss Mittersill became Schäfer's new headquarters and a center for Tibetan and Asian studies where expedition members could be trained.

Beger and Schäfer were both friends and colleagues. They worked side by side in Ancestral Legacy, with Schäfer responsible for its natural sciences sector. According to the historian Michael Kater, they strove to codify their visions and racial ideology into a form of "Aryan mathematics," joining "ancestral legacy" and "glacial cosmogony" into a combination of racial and low-temperature studies. Schäfer visited Dachau in his capacity as a Tibet expert to observe medical experiments conducted on prisoners by SS doctors to measure human reactions to freezing temperatures and altitude. Beger visited Auschwitz in June 1943 to conduct anthropological measurements. He was particularly interested in Mongols and Tibetans, but that interest may have exceeded ancestral legacy.

In the Nuremberg Trials after World War II, Schäfer gave the following deposition: "Himmler had some very strange ideas. He wanted to prove the Nordic race had come down directly from the skies. They all believed in glacial cosmogony. Needless to say, the whole thing was quite unscientific . . . and so far-fetched that it is hard to believe. They all dabbled in the occult."

Did they perceive the Himalayan snowman as a "cold-resistant Proto-Aryan"? This would explain why the Nazis canceled a Tibetan exhibit that was to be held in Salzburg in 1941, an exhibit that included two stuffed Tibetan bears. If the Aryans, as Himmler imagined, were of glacial provenance, and if Proto-Aryans were still to be found in Tibet, then stuffed bears did not fit the Nazi concept of the snowman.

The theory of glacial cosmogony posited that all cosmic energy springs from the clash between ice and fire. It was a popular theory at the time, believed by more than the largely ignorant Nazi leadership. Himmler was convinced that it proved the divine origin of the Aryan race. The yeti may have been the reason for his mandate that the Tibetan data be kept secret.

Jens Sparschuh, in his novel *Der Schneemensch* (The Snowman), gives this idea a fictitious twist. Meyer, his Schäfer-like protagonist, says, "There is evidence that suggests that the so-called Abominable Snowman might well be racially (and I *am* treading carefully here) related to us. In his evolution, he might well have branched off from our ancestors and struck roots in the ice of the

Himalayas, where he survived the passage of the centuries undamaged."

Schäfer described Tibet as a Shangri-la, a place that preserved the purity of species. "Sequestered from the world by high mountain ranges," it was "an almost hermetically sealed area of retreat for forms of life long extinct elsewhere." And he also perceived the Tibetan cult of the dead—"vultures lift the dead back into the skies"—as an Indo-Germanic ritual.

Schäfer concluded that from a zoological standpoint the yeti could only be a Tibetan bear, and he limited himself to this view. As Sparschuh writes of his character Meyer: "He dashes though Tibet, his rifle slung over his shoulder, and can't wait to fire. But as for the primeval ancestor, he's totally off the mark. That was never his specialty."

An enthusiastic scientist and the son of an influential industrialist, Schäfer doubtless didn't regard National Socialism with an unfavorable eye. But as a cosmopolitan man with international connections, he couldn't have thought much of Himmler's ideas of ancestral legacy. However, without the support of Himmler—the SS *Reichsführer*—expeditions abroad would have been impossible during that era. So Schäfer adjusted to the political situation, and Himmler used Tibet to prove his theories about glacial cosmogony. Schäfer may not have seen Tibet as a sanctuary for a proto-Aryan race in which a priestly caste had created subterranean realms, but he did view it as the cradle of humanity. And he knew how to place Tibet and himself in the center of things. With movies, exhibitions, books, and articles, he managed to bring this mysterious and magical land closer to the German people by bringing it into the Third Reich's sphere of interest.

"Tibet Schäfer," as both his critics and admirers called him, would have been pleased with a news flash that arrived in the summer of 1996. In Central Asia, at Lop Nor, south of the Tarim basin, mummies of corpses were found that looked German or Irish. Sun symbols were buried with them. Was this proof that the homeland of the Indo-Germans was precisely where Schäfer's former colleagues had presumed it to be?

Schäfer's interest in Tibet lasted his entire life. He visited the fourteenth Dalai Lama in Dharamsala, wrote treatises about the yeti, and tirelessly tried to educate the local population about their fauna. In 1959, during an expedition, he wrote, "About a hundred yards away from us, three snorting, shaggy giants towered up before us. Snarling, they rose on their hind legs as if they were about to charge. . . . I could not convince my party that they were not Abominable Snowmen but just regular bears—animals that were quite harmless, really."

On another occasion, Schäfer identified what his Tibetan porters thought was a snowman as a *lungomba,* one of the mystics who cross the Tibetan highlands alone. "He wasn't a Tibetan," wrote Schäfer, "but an Indian fakir from Siliguri on the southern edge of the Himalayas." He was heading for Urga in Mongolia, a two-thousand-mile beeline "through the deepest ravines on earth, over the Himalayas, the Trans-Himalayas, the Kunlun Mountains, through snow-covered, desolate high plateaus, and the Gobi Desert."

Schäfer rightly surmised that yeti legends were tightly interwoven with "ancient Chinese legends of the mighty ape king." These legends told of the bloody wars between armies of humans and apes, who even today fight each other in Chinese opera. Schäfer admitted that he was unable to "sway the natives from their yeti beliefs," but could never understand how the yeti myth could live on after his conclusion that they were bears.

It didn't help that some of his colleagues were willing to entertain stranger conclusions.

The anthropologist C. F. von Haimendorf believed what the Sherpas told him of the "terrible yeti." The Austrian ethnologist R. Nebesky-Wojkowitz, who lived for three years among the mountain dwellers of Sikkim and Tibet, reported that while local accounts of yeti sightings might point to Schäfer's bears, the yetis seemed to hold a deeper significance for these people.

In addition to glacial cosmogony and ancestral legacy, there were other ideas from the lunatic fringe. One letter I received defined the yeti as a cross between an ice bear and Cro-Magnon man: "The ice bears were a sort of domestic pet and were vegetarians. They lived peaceably with Cro-Magnon men, much the way dogs today live with modern man. Ice bears and Cro-Magnon men slept together in tents and caves, which resulted in the creation of the yeti. From 50,000 B.C. to 20,000 B.C., there were twelve thousand yetis living peaceably alongside Cro-Magnon man. Cro-Magnon man died out, and modern man began hunting yetis, who sought refuge in the regions of snow and ice."

Although my statements concerning the yeti (often grossly mis-quoted) remained, I thought, dispassionate, my critics became increasingly vocal. Nobody seemed to want to listen to what I was actually saying. I realized that this might well still be the case even if I furnished irrefutable proof of the yeti's source.

I spent the winter of 1992–93 in Nepal. First I went to Solo Khumbu, where a rumor was going round that a young woman had been raped by a yeti. Later, in Mustang, people told me of the exis-tence of a pelt and skeleton of a *mete,* the local name for the yeti, but no one knew where exactly these relics could be found. Foot-prints had been seen in Tsarog Gompa in the summer of 1992, a day's ride from Lo Mantang, but had been blown away by the wind. In Tsarang I heard that the hunters of a former chief known locally as the King of Mustang had once killed a yeti. People said that it had been shot after walking upright a couple of hundred yards, carrying a yak calf under its arm.

There was heavy snow in Dolpo that year and I managed to get only as far as Lake Phoksundo, where a group of young lamas spent the winter completely cut off from the outside world. They were shy, their faces so grimy that they could easily have been mistaken for "wild men."

In the Rolwaling region I climbed up to the meadows of Naa, where the rare "blue bears" reputedly lived. More than half of the two dozen or so huts by the bend in the river were empty, their walls crumbling and their roofs caving in. I went to the huts out of whose chimneys or windows I saw smoke and asked for potatoes and a place to spend the night, but was shooed away. The hovels looked desolate; the people had their hands full just trying to stay alive. They were building dikes against the floods. Men and children stood by the edge of the water while women carried stone blocks weighing hundreds of pounds on their backs. This torrent was the Rolwaling Sherpa's nemesis. The floods had been coming at shorter and shorter intervals, washing away fields, walls, bridges, and dikes.

When I asked people in the village of Beding about the yeti, they merely laughed. Even the yetis had abandoned this desolate place. People who lay awake night after night during the rainy season were not listening for the call of the yeti or the howls of the wolves. The rain, and the river that could rise in a single night and destroy everything—that was all they were thinking of.

The old people told me that twenty or more years earlier—in those Decembers when snow was heavy—a *tshute* (yet another name for the yeti) could sometimes be seen crossing from one valley to another. "On two legs, sometimes on four," one added. None had themselves seen the *tshute*. I said that perhaps that meant none were left. Not true, they responded. Footprints were found in 1991 in the Melung territory.

Beding was a place without rumors. The yeti existed only in old people's imaginations and in the questions of a dwindling number of tourists. Nobody had time to embellish old legends.

"Yetis?" A toothless old man laughed. "An invention of the Sherpas over in Khumbu, who keep the climbers and tourists entertained with new tales of love-crazed females dragging off their prey into caves. All tales for those who imagine the Himalayas to be what they are not."

I only had to look out the window to see what the old man meant. Our Western view of the Himalayas had become so skewed that we were no longer able even to take notice of reports from serious scientists. We were still in the thrall of sensationalized accounts from a century before. In his 1890 book *The Land of the Lamas,* W. Rockhill writes "of frightening, hairy wild men with long, shaggy hair, who have been known to hurl rocks at travelers!" And W. Filchner, who traveled extensively throughout eastern Tibet in the period after World War One, describes the bears, which the natives feared as much as they did the yetis, in his 1925 book *Tschung Kul:* "Both the Chinese and the Tibetans are quite frightened of bears. In the spoken tongue, Master Bruin is known as 'strong man' or 'wild-haired mountain man.' His appearance fills the natives with indescribable fear. Before I left for Tibet, I was warned that I would encounter bears with gigantic eyes of fire. A single bear was more powerful than three strong men put together!"

The following day I began my descent into the valley. Spring had arrived and rhododendron bushes and orchids were in bloom. The jagged foothills of Gaurisankar towered into the clear morning sky. As I turned to look back at the wintry landscape, something startled me. In the middle of the fresh greenness of a barley field stood a dung-smeared scarecrow made of wood, rags, and scraps of fur.

9

FOOTPRINTS IN THE SNOW

Go back to your yeti!" shouted an old man as he passed me on the street in the town where I live in Austria. My daughter Magdalena was with me. "Why do people yell at you about the yeti?" she asked me solemnly.

"I don't know," I replied, "maybe they don't like what I say about it."

"But it's none of their business!" she exclaimed, still upset.

"Yes, it is. The yeti belongs to anyone who has heard of it, and no one wants to give up the picture they have in their head. Everyone sees it their own way."

"The real yeti couldn't care less, right?"

"Absolutely right. The yeti is really thick-skinned. He has no idea that half the world is thinking about him," I said as we drove home.

I was partly to blame for the ridicule I got whenever the yeti question came up. After all, I kept making statements and giving interviews. But the sometimes hostile reactions were beginning to have an effect on my family. It wasn't easy for them that so many people thought me crazy. The media generally portrayed me as obsessed—an undignified state of affairs for a man of fifty. I would reply that I was more obsessed with achieving my goal on the Nanga Parbat and in Antarctica than I was with the yeti. Still, I was keenly aware that to prove that I had not been hallucinating when I saw a yeti that day in 1986, I had to photograph one. I faced a paradox. The yeti had to be found—but its mystery left intact.

Reports of ice monsters and legendary creatures grew more numerous every year. The Russians had sounded the alarm after a snowmanlike creature had suddenly appeared on the border between Siberia and China. A state-owned Chinese travel agency offered $50,000 for the capture of a live yeti. Top dollars were on offer to anyone who could produce photographs and videos of the abominable snowman, or even just tufts of hair and bits of dung. A dead yeti could bring a small fortune. I was still receiving new theories from cryptozoologists. Some continued to claim the yeti was a *gigantopithecus.* "Where else could all the footprints in the snow have come from?" one asked. "They couldn't all have been fakes." Almost all the yeti researchers were certain that we were dealing with a so-called endemic species, a missing link between *Homo erectus* and *Homo habilis*—despite the extreme unlikelihood a primitive hominid could have survived in the eternal snows.

For my part, I was skeptical about the skeptics who claimed that yetis had only ever been sighted by white foreigners. They also claimed that the foreigners' descriptions of the yeti were suspiciously similar to the basic image of the mythological yeti—tall and hairy, with gigantic feet and teeth as long as human fingers. For this reason I found particularly interesting a Tibetan woman's account of tracks she and some friends had found while visiting the Karnali region in western Nepal:

We lived for a long time in a village in which the natives spoke of "wild men" as if they were an everyday matter. We were introduced to a local guide who finally took us to see some footprints. We trekked for two weeks, at times through "forbidden" regions into which natives had only entered in the past two years. The prints we saw in the snow at an altitude of 17,500 feet were about a foot long. They definitely could not have been those of a human being. And anyway, in these cold temperatures the natives wear boots. Not too far from there, about two days' walk, in an area where hardly anyone has ever gone, we came across similar prints leading to a desolate valley. . . . Our guide and the other natives were convinced that these were the footprints of a "wild man."

Chönzom Emchi, the author of this account, is Tibetan but has lived in Switzerland for many years. So convinced was she that she had been on the track of an actual yeti that she could not grasp the questions I put to her about the creature's mythological background. Traditional wisdom, which had fled the country with the Dalai Lama, was beginning to die out. A new generation of Tibetan intellectuals such as Emchi was emerging. They had studied at Western universities and lived abroad, and because of that the Tibetan mind-set was becoming foreign to them. Outside the context of the old nature religion, the yeti was reduced to the merely zoological. It was clear once again that the mystery of the yeti would only be solved in the Central Asian highlands.

In the summer of 1996, I traveled with some friends from Chengdu to Lhasa. Rather than taking the southern route, which tourists had been taking for the past two decades, we traveled north, where Ernst Schäfer had trekked with the second Brooke Dolan expedition. Trucks often needed as long as two weeks to make that trip. We gave ourselves more time than that, since we wanted to get off the beaten track.

From the start of our trip, we were alarmed by the extent of deforestation undertaken by the Chinese. Yak cadavers were piled on the roadside. The stocks of animals had grown—in Kham they had more than doubled since 1959—and many thousands had died of starvation during the winter. Forests near roads were being plundered by Chinese units drilling for mineral resources. It was thought that Tibet might have the richest uranium resources in the world, as well as rich deposits of chrome, borax, lithium, and iron ore. It is also true that since the Chinese had begun their occupation of Tibet, half of the country's arable land has become irrigated. Small power stations have even been built. But nature's balance has been thrown off. The Chinese had forgotten that yaks need food in winter.

Over the centuries, Tibetans have learned to survive in a habitat in which subsistence seems impossible to outsiders, and with time every inch of Tibet developed its own legends. Gods and spirits grew among the streams, the clouds, and the mountains. Belief in them helped Tibetans bear poverty, suffering, and privation—and inspired them to build gigantic monastic fortresses for their monks. The people accepted every hardship—winter storms and droughts—as god-sent. Over the centuries a view of life developed, one that taught Tibetans to endure hunger and extreme temperatures, and to cover great distances on foot. Religion governed and defined life, and without the monks and the aristocracy they have proven incapable of class struggle.

High above the gorges of Sichuan and Yunnan, where Chinese and Tibetans have lived side by side since time immemorial, lay the homeland of the yak nomads. These East Tibetan tribes live isolated from each other between high mountain ridges. They speak their own dialects, wear their own costumes, and have developed a distinct building style tailored to the climate and altitude.

We set up camp for a few days on the shores of Yulung Lhantso, the "Divine Lake" located at the foot of some glacial granite mountains. In the kitchen tent I overheard local herdsmen and our porters engaged in a heated discussion. Though I could not understand everything that was being said, the word *chemo* kept cropping up. I listened closely.

When I asked what the fuss was about, the local herdsmen told me that two days earlier a chemo had been seen farther up between the lake and the glacier.

"There have always been chemos here," one said.

"Which of you saw this animal?" I asked.

The men looked at each other and shook their heads: "None of us." A man named Lopsang, who lived farther up the shore, had told them. His tent was only about an hour's walk away.

As I was getting my backpack ready, a hunchbacked old man came over and asked if I was interested in seeing a yeti hand. I told him I was and asked where it was. At a relative's house, the old man replied—about a day's ride. I asked him if he'd be willing to bring it to me and introduce me to the man who'd killed it.

"He's been dead some forty years," replied the old man.

"How old is this hand?" I asked.

"I have no idea. It's always been there."

The hunchbacked man rode off on his pony, disappearing behind a hill.

The day had grown warmer by the time I arrived in the nomad camp. A few yak-hair tents stood in a meadow that sloped gently down toward the lake. Lopsang was a gaunt man of indeterminable age who lived with his family in a tent right below the edge of the forest. He immediately invited me in to stay. He also confirmed that he often saw chemos in this region, and that he had seen one only a few days earlier.

"Where?" I asked.

"There," he said, pointing far out into the valley with a stick.

"When?"

"If we go out at night, I'm certain we'll see him."

Powdery snow lay on the ridges higher up, but the slopes below were bare. The narrow strip of forest above the tents looked desolate in the light of the setting sun. I worried about getting lost, wandering around this mountain wilderness in the middle of the night.

Lopsang invited me into his tent, gave me some furs to put under my sleeping bag, then offered me some *tsampa*. These highland yak-hair tents are far more comfortable than the smoke-filled stone huts farther down in the valleys; they consist of a single room with only a single opening for light and ventilation. There is little furniture other than a single oven made of clay and stone placed along the longest side. Everything is set up simply and efficiently. When the sun sets, the living area can easily be turned into a spacious sleeping area.

I sat on the right-hand side, the part reserved for visitors and men, while the women and children returned one by one from milking, obviously chilled to the bone, and gathered on the left. There were no beds. At night, everyone covered themselves in clothes and blankets. Then the whole family huddled for warmth under a single large cover of sewn sheepskins. While the children slept, Lopsang and I began to talk.

"What does this chemo look like?" I asked him.

"Bigger than an ape and very strong."

"Are there any apes in these parts?"

"No," Lopsang said. "There are no apes here."

"Chemos are shy, right?"

"Yes, but after a cold winter they lose some of that shyness, and one can watch them."

I understood what he meant. Even mountain hares are more trusting in the spring, and many of the larger animals venture closer to man's environment. Magpies, ravens, and finches almost act like domestic animals.

"There's a hermit living nearby who is close to chemos," Lopsang told me.

"Are chemos yetis?" I blurted out.

He stared at me blankly. It was a foolish question. As far as Lopsang was concerned, a chemo was a chemo. It only turned into a yeti down in the valleys where people were unfamiliar with it. This jagged country is not only rich in its variety of animal species, but its natives also tend to see the same animal with different eyes. Tibet's fauna and flora have tended to create variants. This is particularly true in the case of rare animals. Moreover, locals consider animals that evolved early, such as pandas, takins, and musks, to be more than mere animals. Cut off from the outside world by harsh mountain ranges, these species have survived by being highly adaptable—and they have become not only reality to the people living among them but the stuff of legends, legends fueled by the extreme isolation in which these people live.

I fell asleep. Lopsang woke me up a few hours later. He was already standing outside the tent, ready to go, sliding his arm-long sword between his belt and his animal-skin coat. He went on ahead to the edge of the forest, a dark patch beneath the snow-covered slopes. I followed behind him throughout the night—along cattle paths and clearings, through marshes and underbrush. Every so often Lopsang would stop and listen to the silence or sniff the ground. We found dens, dung, and in the morning, after Lopsang had started talking again, a few footprints in the snow.

"Chemo," he said, pointing at the prints. I would have mistaken them for human, had they not been so large. I took a picture of them. There was no sign of claws. If this giant had been walking on all fours, I told Lopsang, he would have had to place his hind legs with each step into the prints made by his forepaws.

"That's exactly what he does," Lopsang replied.

I took photographs of the footprints from different angles. They were fresh.

"How did he get away from us?" I asked Lopsang.

"What do you mean? He went this way!"

"I know, but I want to see him with my own eyes."

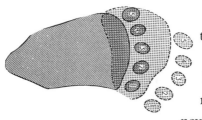

Lopsang smiled. "He'd frighten the living daylights out of you."

"One can never find a chemo," he added after a while. "Either you run into one by chance, or you never get to see one. He always appears at night, and only when you least expect it."

"But he steals your animals!"

"Yes, at night, and mostly in the fog and rain, when we can't see a thing."

"What about shooting him?"

"We don't have any rifles, and by the time we round up men with clubs and knives, he's long gone."

"What does he eat?"

"His favorite food is goat. But he'll eat anything: roots, ants, weeds, berries, marmots, yaks, sheep."

Lopsang bade me farewell near the hermit's settlement on the other side of the lake and returned to his family. I climbed up a steep path to some huts that were wedged in a rift high in the rock face. A solitary man was sitting on the ground staring at me.

For a long time the hermit said nothing. Matted tufts of hair hung down his shoulders. His face was darker than that of the nomads. Eventually he got up and led me to his small meditation chamber, in which there was a row of artifacts: a skull set in silver, a flute made of human bone, a drum covered with human hide. Back outside, he told me that a few days before he had seen a chemo mother playing with her child, and that he had spoken with her. Then he took my binoculars and gazed endlessly at the split peak of the Chunama, a holy mountain located at the far end of the valley. I took a look, too: between the split ridges of the mountain peak was an outcropping of rock that looked like a meditating Buddha pointing into the sky.

When I returned to the camp, I asked about the chemo hand

Lopsang had mentioned to me earlier and was shown a paw—
a rotting, worm-eaten thing I immediately identified as that of a bear.

"This is just a bear paw," I muttered, and then began haggling
over the price.

"It's a chemo hand!" the woman who owned it argued. She began to walk away, a tactic no doubt intended to make me buy it. I
realized from the way the nomads were acting that in their eyes it was
far more than a bear paw. Beneath the sparse bristles, the smoke-
dried paw did vaguely resemble a human hand. Fake or not, what I
was being offered was the yeti myth itself. After hesitating for a few
moments, I agreed to the woman's price, wrapped the thing in a
piece of paper, put it in a plastic bag, and packed it into my rucksack.

In the weeks that followed we trekked and drove through the
intense light of the endless Tibetan uplands at altitudes of fourteen thousand to seventeen thousand feet. Not a bush in sight, not
a tree, nothing. During the day, warm air rose into the deep blue
skies, while in the evenings bitter-cold winds whipped across the
land. The nights were icy cold. Plants here had only three months
in which to grow, blossom, and wither before the winter storms.
Mammals in Tibet have thicker fur and tougher hair than anywhere
else in the world, protection against the terrible winds and the
extreme fluctuations of temperature. Yaks graze with their backs to
the wind, so that their bushy tails cover part of their body. Chemos,
as nocturnal animals who live high up in the snow regions, would
have to be better equipped than any other animal.

Old men, women carrying their babies on their backs, and children walked the unpaved roads through clouds of dust. We saw them
setting up camps, boiling tea by the roadsides, burning aromatic
herbs, and praying incessantly. These groups of pilgrims, making up
what seemed like one long procession, were all on their way to
Lhasa. Wherever they were, smoke hung in the air.

In one of the wayside villages, I asked a group of Tibetan men whether they had ever seen a chemo. They laughed, studied me carefully, and pointed to the forest.

"Yes," one of them said. "I've seen one hanging in the courtyard of a store. In the bazaar, a few houses down."

I had him take me there. We stopped outside a row of wooden shacks. *Tashi delek!* I called out.

An old man, his face blackened by the mountain sun, stuck his tongue out in welcome as we entered his store. I couldn't follow the conversation, but I heard the words *chemo* and *photograph*. The store owner opened the back door and led us into a dimly lit stockroom. A pelt was hanging on the wall. The air was heavy with the stench of decay and rancid fat. As I lifted the pelt off its hook, a tuft of fur came off in my hand. The Tibetans didn't mind my taking pictures and watched me, smiling. They wanted to know if I wanted to buy it. No, I told them, I just wanted to take pictures.

When I walked out into the street again, I was shivering with excitement. I was certain I had just seen proof of the chemo's existence, and it corresponded with everything that I had long suspected—that it was a rare species of bear. The creature's habitat was mountain valleys lying at altitudes between twelve thousand and eighteen thousand feet. The Sherpas, the sowers of the original yeti myth, had migrated from this very region. The yeti, in other words, was a chemo blown up to mythic proportions. Rather than a mirage, an illusion, a fantasy, or a fable, the yeti had its roots in the close proximity to man of an animal whose behavior remained mysterious.

It was time I observed these animals in their natural habitat.

In the streets of Lhasa, into which daily pour nomads from all over Tibet and the neighboring Chinese provinces of Sichuan, Chinghai, and Sinkiang, the legend of the yeti was everywhere. Many nomads arrive on foot, following treks that can last many months. Wrapped in cloth or yak-hide coats, they walk clockwise around the

Jokhang, the holiest of temples. The Jokhang was over thirteen hundred years old and according to legend had been built over a subterranean lake in which the future could be read. These pilgrims undertake this journey to make themselves worthy of their next reincarnation. Some had come to die.

The pilgrims stayed in Parkor all night, sitting around campfires and praying. They formed small groups around their elders, cooking, eating, and telling stories, while the oldest men fanned the flames with bellows. They poured butter tea into their wooden bowls from a communal pot and kneaded clumps of barley dough. Dogs sat waiting for scraps of food and were thrown bits of fat and meat.

Before continuing our journey, we visited the park at Norbulinka, whose zoo, which lay between the pavilions and willow trees, was a favorite spot for the people of Lhasa. There were monkeys, wildcats, and foxes behind wire netting. And behind a barrier made of finger-thick iron bars were two bears that I was convinced were chemos. Here were not yetis, but the yetis' zoological blueprint.

Some lamas guarding the animals and the park watched me from a distance. The lamas approached when I tried to push my Leica between the iron bars. They weren't about to let me take these momentous pictures of the chemos without a tip.

In the fall of 1996 I returned to Tibet with a German television crew and traveled through western Tibet from Katmandu to the Kailash Mountain and Manasarowar, the holy lake. At the western foot of Kailash we came upon a pilgrim who kept pointing up into the fog and saying *dremong*. I didn't understand his dialect, and only on our return journey did a Tibetan student enlighten me while we were sitting in a caravansary on the high road. He wrote down the following formula: *dremong = chuti = yeti = miti*.

When I got back to Katmandu to continue my research, I was careful about pronouncing *chemo* to sound more like *dremong*. But the Khampas did not seem to understand me, so I went back to saying *yeti,* though I was sick of the word. I came across lots of tourists on the streets of Katmandu and caught snippets of their conversation, mostly in languages I did not understand. *Yeti* seemed common to them all.

When I returned to my office in Austria after my Kailash trip, Ruth, my secretary of many years, handed me a letter from Kodak. "The roll of Kodachrome slide film you sent us for development was damaged during delivery," the letter read. "Unfortunately, we will be unable to develop it. As a gesture of goodwill, we are happy to enclose a new roll."

The damaged roll had contained shots of the prints in the snow. My clearest proof to date had been destroyed.

10

WHITE HEAD
AND BLACK GIANT

In April 1997, accompanied by a guide and interpreter from Lhasa named Karma, I drove through the tea plantations, rice paddies, and cornfields of Chengdu in Sichuan to the Tibetan highlands. We traveled by Jeep over the Ala Pass, which yak caravans have crossed for centuries, bringing tea to Tibet, and made our way west from one trading post to the next. The Red Guards entered Tibet by this route after the Kuomintang had built a road to Yinthum Lhatso. The Khampas did not manage to repel the Chinese there, and the Red Guard in their tanks, fighter jets, and trucks quickly moved on Lhasa.

There was deep snow in the high passes between Kanze and Dege, and therefore constant danger from avalanches, but we made it through. Along the whole route we came across Chinese personnel fixing roads and drainage ditches, but no one tried to stop us. My luck ran out in Dege, where the police came after me. The Chinese didn't want a European traveling alone through Tibet. While Karma was negotiating with the local authorities, I stayed at his uncle's, with whom I discussed the situation in Tibet.

"Everything is growing scarcer," he complained, "compassion, the wealth of mantras, creed. The ceremonies, too."

"But the Dalai Lama is being supported by the West."

"I know, but that's bad. Now all Tibetans expect help from the West."

"Don't people understand what's going on?"

"We have too little political education."

"What about Lamaism?"

"That's losing ground, too. Buddhism is orienting itself to the West."

When I asked Karma's uncle about chemos, he told me a story about one who had stolen a pig right in the middle of Dege. "The pig must have weighed sixty-five pounds. He just picked it up and ran off with it. This was back in 1977, I think."

"And what does it look like?"

"People say he has an ugly face, and when he grabs a goat, he injures many others while he's at it."

"What do the Chinese call this creature?"

"*Ren shung.* We call him *chemong* or *chemo.*"

"And what's a *migiö?*"

"*Migiö* means 'standing bear.' In dialect it is also known as *ne-te,* which means 'bear man.' "

"What is the giant panda bear called?"

"*Shumo* in Chinese."

"So, what is this chemong?"

"He's not a bear, not as far as we Tibetans are concerned."

"Why not?"

"Chemongs carry their children on their backs and take them over rivers. And they whistle by blowing out air, like this." He showed me what he meant. "They play among themselves and yap like dogs. *Tom* is the word for bear. Tom are quicker, smaller, and almost always walk on all fours."

"Are migiö and chemongs one and the same?"

"No. The Chinese use *migiö* for 'wild man.' But no one has ever seen one of those here in Tibet."

"Chemongs though, have been seen?"

"Yes, in the fall they can even be seen in the fields, and in the spring they eat freshly planted potatoes. They can't see very well, and when people come too close, they attack—out of fear, I think. They'll stand up, look, threaten. They also stand on their hind legs when they are angry or on the lookout. We call their children *tsetu.*"

"The chemo is like a human being, only larger," Karma's uncle continued. "He has small eyes and a pointed mouth. He is different from other animals. He kills with his hands and has feet like human feet, but without the defined heel. He will throw stones at dogs, and they avoid him. He always throws the stones backward. In May, chemos will come out after sundown and hunt for marmots. That's when they are easy to find. But in the fall you can only find them high up in the mountains."

"What about in the winter?"

"I don't know. Maybe some hibernate, but not all."

After extensive negotiations with the police, we were allowed to drive down to the Yangtze River and up into the Mesha Valley. The road came to an end between a few villages of hovels. The slopes above the valley were covered with brush. A path wound its way up and we followed it toward the Dora pastures. We camped at one of the wintering places, approximately thirteen thousand feet up, with some nomads who keep their yaks, sheep, and goats here from November to May. In June they move higher up to the edge of the glacier, taking with them their tents, animals, and children.

After a five-hour trek we came upon a wide valley. The Dora pastures lay before us, and they were not what we had imagined—they seemed to consist of a few dung heaps, a pen for the animals, and two huts of clay and wood, all surrounded by a brush enclosure.

After a few days the excitement I had felt in the valley about seeing a chemo in the wild gave way to disillusionment. We found no chemo nor heard chemo calls. But I was prepared to be patient, to wait weeks if necessary. I didn't have to.

One day, Karma and I set out before dusk and climbed a narrow, overgrown path until we reached a clearing high above the valley. We crouched down and trained our binoculars on the steep mountainsides on the other side of the river valley. The peaks above it were still lit by the sun, while the woods below were pitch-black.

"Chemo!" Karma suddenly whispered.

"Where?" I asked.

"He is large and dark and has a white head. I think he has children," Karma said in a hushed voice.

"Where?" I whispered again. Karma pointed at a narrow ridge between some high conifers. Holding my binoculars tight in both hands, my elbows propped on my knees, I scoured the rocks. I couldn't see a thing.

"There! Under those large trees! You can clearly see his white head!"

By the time I finally saw the animal—it was leaning its forepaw on a tree trunk, gazing at a rhododendron forest—it was turning away to climb up the slope through the underbrush. It crossed the steep escarpment quite calmly, the sun at its back, disappeared behind a tree, and then reappeared one last time. It had a massive body and a white head. We named him White Head.

We returned to the camp and announced our sighting to some young women herding goats. They didn't show the slightest reaction to our news. Each had her set duties, and seeing chemos, after all, was an everyday occurrence in these parts. Which was also why, when they had finished milking, they locked the goats in the stable near their own cavelike quarters.

We set out the following morning to stalk White Head and found tracks, hair, and dung. We also found some clumps of fur and the skull of a young takin. We climbed a steep, rocky slope and found some more footprints, filling us with excitement. White Head had walked over this ground. This was his path, his domain.

The terrain became so steep that we had to start climbing, keeping our eyes glued on the next step. We finally arrived at a resting spot, a jumble of gnarled trees and jagged rock.

Here only the chemo could prevail. White Head's lair had to be somewhere above us—a hideaway between abyss and heaven.

We climbed for hours. He was nowhere to be found.

When we returned, the young women in the meadow wanted to know if we had at least seen the children.

"What children?" I asked.

"The chemo's children." Locals referred to their cubs as children, stressing their human attributes.

The people of this region described the chemo exactly as the Sherpas did the yeti: nocturnal, usually a loner, with fur that could be either dark or light, depending on its age. He often walked on two legs, almost as upright as a human being. His dung looked like human excrement, though it contained the crushed bones and fur of rodents. These animals were shy and intelligent and lived both above and below the timberline. They usually stayed below the snow line, even in midsummer, and only ventured across the glaciers when necessary. They were often seen or heard near villages, particularly in the spring or during the long winter months.

Two days later, a blanket of new snow covered the ground. I hoped that it would stick, making it easier to find tracks. Karma and I climbed down into the valley, then zigzagged our way up the opposite slope. We found some footprints, a few freshly dug holes, and some more dung, but nothing else.

In the afternoon we came across five men carving up a yak. They told us a giant chemo had killed it, then buried it so that he could come back for the carcass whenever he was hungry. We found his gigantic footprints close by, and dung. The men sold us a chunk of the yak carcass. We reburied it where the chemo had hidden it, then we lay in wait. We waited half the night, initially about a hundred yards away from the bait, and later, when it started raining, moved closer. The chemo didn't appear. Disappointed and wet, we trudged through the rain and snow in the darkness back to the camp, which we reached after midnight.

The following morning, some children from a neighboring valley told us they had seen a "black giant" a few days before. They described him as terrifying but not manlike. Judging by the way they spoke and waved their arms, their story seemed plausible. They showed us the spot where they had encountered him, and it wasn't far from where we had left our bait. The meat was gone. Obviously, two chemos were afoot in the area, White Head and (as we now called him) Black Giant. We descended into valleys and climbed to the upper edges of the forests. Every evening we scoured the undergrowth beneath the high pastures.

During a thunderstorm we found footprints in the forest that were probably those of Black Giant. He had obviously been hunting a yak. His prints were over a foot long, and there were skid marks on the mossy earth.

The next morning we headed east. We followed mountain trails, crossed a pass, and entered a valley where we came upon a group of huts in the fog. I thought at first that the light was playing tricks on our eyes, but as we neared there came the smell of manure and rancid butter. We entered one of the huts, were offered *tsampa* and butter tea, and stayed until the sun broke through the fog, at which point we set off again.

Karma told me that his father, Anjam, lived a few clearings farther up, by the edge of the forest, in a tiny hut of wood and clay. He had left his family in the valley and was leading a hermitlike existence. Anjam was known as a chemo expert, and when I met him, I discovered why. The old man told us of an incident that had occurred the previous year. As he spoke, he grew increasingly animated:

"One night, in pitch-black darkness, I was suddenly jolted from my sleep. A chemo was banging his fist so hard against the wall that the whole hut was shaking. Three arm-thick logs cracked. I started yelling with terror, hoping to raise the neighbors. He wouldn't go away. He kept rattling my door. When he couldn't open it, he began tearing a hole into the wall next to it. It was only when I pointed my flashlight through the hole at his face that he ran off into the forest."

"Was he alone?" I asked.

"Yes, he was alone."

"Are chemos always alone?"

"No," Anjam replied. "About an hour from here, I watched three chemos dancing together."

"What do you mean, dancing?"

"You know, the way children dance when they are playing."

"But otherwise, are chemos loners?"

"They sometimes hunt in groups. One time they drove a yak calf to the river." Anjam pointed east, toward the valley. "They killed it and ate it."

"Do they kill people, too?"

"They don't usually eat human flesh. Only when they are startled do they become dangerous for us. The bad thing is that chemos know everything. They can tell when there are no people in a mountain pasture. Then they come—in the middle of the night, of course—and tear a hole in the roofs of the sheds to get at the goats that are usually tied in the middle of the pens. Then they grab one and disappear. Chemos have magical powers, there's no doubt about it. Black magic. They know everything. They watch us very carefully from up there, maybe from a rock or something, and know who is guarding the huts and when. You can't see them, but they can see you."

As far as the natives were concerned, the forests and the impenetrable underbrush belonged to the chemo alone. When I visited a family living in a hollow higher up the mountain, I learned how wary local people were of all things foreign. Even before we reached the wooden barrier around the camp, we heard the dull barking of the Tibetan dogs, waiting to chase away any strangers—human or otherwise.

We were gazing at the mountain slope on the other side of the valley—where we could see our tents, tiny dots of color—when a man approached. I asked him if there were any chemo caves nearby. He told us that he knew one and said to follow him. We descended into the valley and then climbed another fifteen hundred feet up the mountain. I did the last leg of the trek on my own and found an outcrop of rock the height of church tower. At the center of it was a cave strewn with hay. It was empty. The area all around was so steep that I didn't want to try looking any farther. Suddenly something shot out of the underbrush and dashed off. I couldn't tell what it was.

Late that evening we climbed down the slope and discovered another cave. Nochar, one of Karma's brothers, had joined us and was intent on finding the Black Giant. Again we found nothing but footprints. We perched on a rock spur and stared at the surrounding forests and ravines until we were shivering with cold and couldn't sit still anymore. We headed back to camp in the dim moonlight, without using our flashlights—we didn't want to irritate the chemos.

I still didn't have a photograph of the creature, and its tracks were now lost in the blackness of the forests. I trudged toward the camp, tired and feeling weighed down by my backpack, which was heavy with cameras and night-vision equipment.

With each nightly march back to camp, through torrents, mud, and underbrush, another bit of hope that I would obtain proof of the yeti was chipped away. Each night I would feel that maybe this whole trip to the most remote mountain valleys of eastern Tibet was ridiculous.

But come morning, off I would set again, and after I'd trekked for a few hours my old curiosity would return. It inevitably blossomed into the conviction that I was on the right track.

Karma returned home, but Nochar and I continued our search for White Head and Black Giant. We didn't have a plan for how we would go about photographing a chemo, nor one for what we would do if we encountered one. It wasn't as if we would ambush it. People always said that one could only encounter a chemo by chance. "If you look for him, you will never find him." We were looking for him, but it felt as if he were watching us.

The following morning I woke up sick. I felt so wretched that I had to be helped down the ladder from the roof platform of the hut where I had pitched my tent. I went to the stream to wash. There I sat down on a rock, the bells of the yak herd at my back, frost flowers floating on the water before me. I sat there for a long time, feeling miserable, asking myself what I was doing here.

It was damp and cold, a sunless morning. I stared at the forested slopes. A flock of birds rose above a clearing just below the snow line—vultures! Suddenly my sense of mission came back. I hurried along the path, past the courtyards covered with dry yak dung, to the hovels in the pastures. The vultures were still circling high above the valley. I called Nochar. He pointed at them and picked up the binoculars.

What did this mean? Had a yak been taken or was something lying among the rock ridges, bluffs, and gnarled weeds? The flock of vultures kept hovering above the same spot. Was Black Giant on the prowl?

I was too weak to climb to the edge of the forest, so Nochar went alone. He found a dead yak. It had fallen to its death, Nochar told me when he returned to the camp.

That afternoon, Nochar spotted a chemo on the opposite slope. He thought it might be White Head. Although I wasn't feeling much better, I set off with him. We must have startled the animal, for it disappeared into the underbrush. We waited, listening to the birds, until dusk turned to darkness. It became so quiet that the whole world seemed to shudder at the sound of a cracking branch. We stayed late into the night in tense anticipation, then set off back to camp.

The following morning we climbed a ledge that jutted out far into the valley. This time we had a plan: to lure a chemo with the sharp odor of yak bones. We tied the bones to a tree, low enough so it could reach them, and hid about fifty yards away behind a knotted spruce tree, from which we had a good view.

Birds started arriving, then more birds, but that was all.

Dusk came and the sky had grown cloudy and dark when we suddenly heard some noises. On the opposite slope was a chemo with two cubs, their fur streaked with white. They were walking upright, sauntering along, tearing out roots, throwing chunks of earth behind them, seemingly carefree. Because of darkness and distance, I knew any photographs we took of the animals would show little. Again I was left with nothing.

We spent the night in our sleeping bags beneath a tree. We woke the next morning to the din of bird cries. The bones were still there. No footprints were to be seen. Our plan had not worked.

The wind carried every sound up to the mountain ridges and over the edge of the forest in which we sat. We waited for hours, silent, scanning one slope after the other with our binoculars, wondering if silence and vigilance were the right approach.

When we returned to the camp, a passing horseman told us that a chemo mother and child could sometimes be seen in Ono, a mountain pasture in the southeast sector of the valley. They usually came out of the forest at dusk and headed for a stream.

On horseback we crossed the Zodala, a pass located in the far reaches of the valley, and descended the steep slope to Ono, a settlement consisting of a few huts in a ravine.

By now we knew that chemos never came out of the forest before dusk, and we rolled out our sleeping bags in an empty stall next to some horses, who stamped their hooves all night, keeping me awake. When we walked back to the camp the following morning, we had a beautiful view of three mountains on the eastern horizon. But no picture.

Our failure had made me restless. I wanted to climb back up to the ridge from which we had seen the chemo mother and cubs. We set off, taking all our camping equipment with us. On the crest of the ridge we dug a foxhole and then covered it with a tarpaulin, so that we could barely be seen. We got in and waited.

The rain poured down, the night turned cold. The water on the tarpaulin froze. From time to time, I crawled to the edge of the ridge to listen for any noises from the slopes below. A light fog rose from the bottom of the valley and lingered in the branches, coating them with dew. I heard nothing.

When the sun rose, ice crystals glittered on the inside of the tarpaulin. The air had become clear. Objects and sounds could be seen and heard at great distances, as if the thin air at this altitude carried better. We returned to the settlement.

In the days that followed we found tracks, but no chemo. One storm followed upon another. Time and again our tents were almost swept off the hut's roof. Nochar prayed incessantly.

As a last resort I wanted to buy a goat to use as live bait, but everyone in the camp seemed against the idea. At first they promised to provide me one, but then kept stalling. Finally they announced they wouldn't. I should have known that it went against their religious principles. According to Buddhism, all life is sacred. An animal's life could not be sacrificed.

Despite an old foot injury—a fractured heel bone that had never completely healed—that was hobbling me, I went with Nochar to Rege Gompa, a monastery perched high above the valley, a retreat for monks immersed in spiritual exercises. As we approached, young lamas peered discreetly out of windows. Others looked down at us from the roof. They marveled at us as if we were rare animals. We walked past the monastery, and when I looked back, it stood like a fortress perched on the edge of the mountain—behind it towered a peak in the shape of the Matterhorn.

We descended into Babung Gompa, a gigantic palace located on a rock plateau above a village whose whole existence seemed to revolve around sustaining the monks. A feast was being held in the village square. Monks were singing, dancing, and laughing. In Tibet, mystics not only devote themselves to introspection, but cultivate a zest for life. Their beliefs center more around respect for nature's law than around ghosts and demons.

The ten-hour hike had exhausted me and my right foot had become swollen, so we decided to return home. We set off a day earlier than planned, loading the two horses that would carry our baggage back down into the valley. In the afternoon, we arrived in Meshe, from which I had set off on my search a month earlier.

It was by now late May. Before the Jeep came to pick us up, I rode to Sosar Gompa, a monastery where word had it a stuffed chemo was on display. I hoped the monks would let me take a picture. It was raining when I rode off, and it was still raining when I got there. Sosar Gompa had been destroyed during the Cultural Revolution but had been rebuilt. A hundred lamas live there now. Hanging above the *gompa* entrance were two stuffed animals—a yak and a chemo. The chemo's mouth was open, its ears and teeth enlarged, and its glassy eyes stared down at me. It was incredibly large.

I asked the head lama whether I could take a picture. He nodded, and to my amazement a couple of young lamas climbed up a ladder and brought the chemo down from the ceiling. When they placed it upright on the flagstones in the courtyard, the crowd moved a few steps back, and I, too, was startled. The stuffed bear-man was frightening even in death. But I also saw respect in the faces of the monks, women, and pilgrims who were casting shy glances at it.

The bravest man among the villagers picked it up and started dancing with it. The crowd began mumbling, then whistling and howling, which turned into a sort of chant that ebbed and flowed, as man and chemo danced across the courtyard to the beat of clapping hands. They were, I realized, cheering for his daring to take on the yeti, with all that it represented.

The following afternoon I went up into the mountains one last time, hoping to photograph a living chemo. Snow had fallen that morning, and I spent hours searching through the woods, crawling though the wet underbrush. Despite the favorable conditions—there was snow up to fourteen thousand feet—this last search didn't bear fruit either. I found the usual tracks, but nothing else. Snow turned to rain as I descended, and when I got back, everything was caked with mud.

Though lacking the proof I longed to find, I remained convinced that the chemo and the yeti were identical, and that both were more than a bear. Arguing that the yeti was merely a bear was nonsense, as was claiming that the yeti was purely fictitious. The yeti myth is indeed a bear myth, but without the legend surrounding it, the *Ursus arctus* would not have become a yeti, even in Tibet.

That evening, as I sat with Karma's extended family in their kitchen, I felt some satisfaction about the journey, despite its failures. The children had been bathed in my honor—a generous gesture, as mountain dwellers usually submit only to what is absolutely necessary for survival.

The next morning, Karma and I hurried along with a small convoy of porters to the high road, where the Jeep was waiting. While Karma went to say good-bye to his mother, I changed from my hiking boots into sneakers. As I sat there barefoot, the children who had crowded around me suddenly started giggling. I looked up, saw the laughter and amazement in their faces, and immediately realized that I, too, was destined to become a part of a story—and perhaps to find a place in the wall hangings and narratives woven around the yeti.

The children stared at the stubs of my amputated toes and at a footprint I had made in the wet mud. They started jumping around me in a kind of farewell dance. *"Chemo, chemo, chemo,"* they sang, clapping and pointing at my feet.

11

THE PIECES FIT

The story that Karim, a Balti porter, told me in Karakorum (located in Jammu and Kashmir, northern India, the region where K2 is located) in the summer of 1997 sounded so unbeliev-able that initially I didn't give it much thought. The story was about a yeti, or as they call it in Karakorum, a *dremo*.

A long time ago, a dremo abducted a girl in Hushe and car-ried her off to a cave, where he held her captive and fed her. Her brothers looked for her but couldn't find her. Years later, the family's dog found the cave and the girl. When the dog brought the girl's necklace back to the village, her family immediately recognized it. The brothers followed the dog to the cave, where they found their sister and wanted to take her back to the village. Six or seven years had passed since her abduction, and she now had two yeti babies and didn't want to go back to the village. But the brothers forced her to come with them and carried her babies in a basket. When they crossed the glacial torrent near the village, they stopped in the middle of the bridge and dropped the children into the water. The woman became frantic, sobbed, wanted to return to her cave, but they wouldn't let her go. A few days later a dremo appeared, obviously looking for her. The village hunted him down and shot him. The woman died shortly thereafter.

"Where is this cave?" I asked Karim after he'd finished, interested in the parallel between this tale and those told by the Sherpas.

"About a half-hour's walk from the village of Hushe."

"Are any dremos still around?"

"Yes, by the glaciers of Biafo, Hispar, and Pagma. And also in Jilini near Astor, and between Lake Sapara and Ladakh," replied Karim, referring to sites all located near the border between India and Tibet.

"And what do they eat?"

"Everything. Meat, grass, fruit, fresh seedlings, roots. They even kill yaks and goats. Ibex, too."

A few days later while we were camping on the Baltoro Glacier, Karim told me another dremo story:

Once there were two dremos—they were mighty monsters— lying in a cave somewhere in the mountains, hibernating. A hunter seeking refuge in this cave became trapped when an avalanche suddenly blocked up its entrance. The hunter killed one of the dremos so that he would have meat to eat. He spared the other dremo. He covered himself with the fur of the animal he had killed, and for the rest of the winter nestled up to the other dremo for warmth. When spring came, the dremo awoke from hibernation and began digging a tunnel through the snow so that they could get out of the cave. He

kept motioning to the hunter to help him. When they broke
through, the dremo fled into the mountains and the hunter
returned home.

A two-week trek across the ice mountains of Baltoro brought
me to Hushe, where I wanted to see if the cave in Karim's story
really existed. He guided me up a mountain path in the rain and fog,
and there among some rocks was a cave. It was room-sized and
looked exactly the way it had been described in the story. If only I

could find these animals to connect story to reality, yeti to chemo and dremo, the pieces in the puzzle would fit.

Lamaism disappeared in Baltistan, which once lay at the edge of western Tibet, seven hundred years ago. Muslim missionaries converted the people and eradicated all traces of the earlier culture. Only the yeti legend survived, as did an epic about a character named Gesar, a shape-shifter able to transform into a dremo to hoodwink people.

The villagers of Hushe can recite whole passages of this epic from memory. An old man with horrific scars was brought to me. I was told he had been mauled by a dremo. I asked him for his story, but he only stared at me; it was as if he had lost his capacity for speech. I pointed at my nose, eyes, and face, indicating that I wanted him to give me details about the features of the animal that had attacked him. He laughed and tugged at my beard. No eyes, no face? The old man shook his head and walked off.

I drove from Hushe to Skardu through golden barley fields. Snow lay on the mountain slopes and fog settled in the ravines; the rivers were heavy with melted snow. Kapalu was dusty, windy, and busy, as all the larger mountain villages tended to be. I knew that the mountain plateau in the south, between Ladakh, Srinigar, and Astor, would be even hotter, but that was where I had to go. Villagers in these highlands told me that more than a dozen dremos lived there, though I could find no one who had actually seen one. To them the creature was not evil incarnate, but intelligent and cautious, a symbol of cunning and power.

"A dremo watches, thinks, and then makes a decision," a young farmer named Gulam Khan explained to me. Khan was considered the most experienced hunter in the region. I asked him if he had seen one.

"Sure. Just the other day. He threw some stones at me and ran off."

When I asked for more details, Khan replied that the animal was as big as a man, though broader, and that it walked upright. Its cheeks, palms, and the soles of its feet were hairless, but otherwise it was covered in hair. Its feet and toes were humanlike; the big toe was long and formidable. The creature had, said Khan, "broad paws," as well as a large nose and pronounced nostrils.

Clearly, this animal's humanlike behavior had generated the yeti myth in Central Asia and allowed for many—and sometimes divergent—conclusions, but everything that I had learned proved that this animal was neither human nor an anthropoid.

Days later I crossed a deep ravine onto a high plateau that was being grazed only along its edges. I was told that dremos spent winters in these ravines. The inner reaches of the plateau were windy—hot during the day, brutally cold at night. Everything here was reminiscent of the Tibetan high plateau: the vegetation, the expanse, the low-lying skies, the way the light bathed everything.

"What does the dremo eat?" I asked my guides.

"Wild onions, grass, and occasionally a marmot."

"No goats? No yaks?"

"No. He keeps away from the few summer pastures here. The animals there are well guarded."

We set up camp at thirteen thousand feet and the following day climbed higher. I was filled with anticipation. Behind a small ridge, barely a stone's throw away, a dremo was grazing. When it caught our scent, it quickly ducked into a depression and disappeared. I managed to creep toward a second dremo, which was sleeping in a hollow, and took a picture of it just as it jumped up and ran away. It looked just like the chemongs of eastern Tibet, only smaller and less shaggy. Later we saw both of them, mother and child, fleeing down the mountainside. We returned to camp and on our way found marmot holes that had been dug up. We also found some dens.

The few people we ran into told us the same dremo stories I had heard in eastern Tibet about chemos, and in Sherpa country about the yeti—about how they grab small children who don't behave and have their way with women, whom they drag off into the mountains. Dremos were also described to us as dancing bears. Rozi Ali, our guide, told us of an encounter he had had: "The female bear, a mother with two children, rose on her hind legs and was about to attack me. But then she quickly turned round and hurried back to her children. Then, suddenly, she stood upright again and turned around in circles like a dancing bear." Ernst Schäfer had also observed the "merry-go-round whirling" of the Tibetan bear—in both healthy and wounded animals—and saw it as a characteristic of the bears of the Central Asian steppes.

Each day we climbed higher, searching through every hollow we came upon. All we found were freshly dug-up marmot holes.

Dremos, which are called *ish* in Gilgit and *rish* in Urdu, are protected in Pakistan and can live in the mountains undisturbed. Farther down in the valleys they are hunted in winter for their fat, we were told, as well as for their penises, which are cut into pieces and fed to cockerels. After a week the birds are cooked and eaten as an aphrodisiac.

The weather turned hot and dry, hotter and drier than anywhere else in the western Himalayan highlands. For weeks the sky was cloudless and deep blue. As if afraid of losing themselves in its depths, birds flew close to the ground. Soon after sunrise, the horizon started shimmering and the landscape seemed to melt. High on the mountains, where masses of clouds gathered above the peaks of Nanga Parbat, the ice fields were melting. It was July, the dremos' mating season.

One afternoon, after a long trek, we encountered another dremo. He fled when he saw us, but then seemed to stop and rest in a hollow. I approached the spot from behind some ridges so that he wouldn't pick up my scent. Rozi Ali followed me. When I began to climb down to where the animal was sleeping in the grass, Rozi Ali tried to stop me. I broke free of his grasp and came within twenty yards of the animal, where I took some good pictures. Rozi Ali, crouching some way back, begged me to make a run for it. He was sweating with fear.

The animal woke up and looked at me the way a startled child would a stranger. It was a young brown bear. It would only turn into a dremo, chemo, or yeti later, when the local people were providing their version of the encounter.

Rozi Ali had reason to be frightened of these animals. In 1990 he had been in charge of the base camp for an American expedition up the Biafo Glacier in Karakorum. One day, while returning from Askole, where he had been shopping, he came face-to-face with a gigantic bear sitting in the kitchen tent, eating. The bear had already destroyed six tents and was to destroy three more in a camp farther up in the mountains. The animal became increasingly bold. Rozi Ali threw stones at it, but it would not go away. It grew angry and menacing, then disappeared. Rozi Ali pitched a tent on a rock slab near the destroyed camp and tried to get some sleep. The dremo returned at about two in the morning and started ransacking the campsite again, eating the provisions that Rozi Ali had brought from Askole. At his wit's end, Rozi Ali took his flashlight and shone it into the creature's face. Nothing happened. The two of them simply stood there, trying to stare each other down. Finally they both backed away.

This drama between Rozi Ali and the bear went on for an entire week, until there were no provisions left and both of them became furious. Rozi Ali went to Askole to get a rifle and came back to the camp at around four in the afternoon intending to shoot the animal. It was nowhere to be found. He waited, searched, prayed, searched again, waited some more. It was evening when the bear came back. After being shot once, it ran away on two legs, but when Rozi Ali hit it with a second shot, it came back. The fifth shot, a shot to the head, finally killed the frenzied, snarling animal.

In Askole, located below the Biafo Glacier, the dremo is thought of as a snowman. But both Hias Rebitsch and Heinrich Harrer, two Austrian mountaineers who have traveled extensively through the regions between the Himalayas and Karakorum, were of the same opinion as I, that the brown bear and the yeti were the same thing. The British adventurer H. W. Tilman described the footprints he found in the upper reaches of the Biafo Glacier as dremo tracks, though he was hesitant about ascribing them to a bear. He reported there were no wild animals of any kind in the area, nor any grazing grounds, and that the nearest village lay over forty miles away. Tracks that Tilman found at a lower altitude he classified as bear tracks.

We saw only one more dremo during our trip to Kashmir. It was running away on two legs. From a distance it looked uncannily like a wild man.

Yeti is a collective term for all the monsters of the Himalayas, real or imagined. It is the abominable snowman, that Western fantasy, as well as the chemo and dremo. My perspective was no longer Western. I did not believe yetis were relics of a prehistoric anthropoid species that had managed to survive undetected. The yeti was a living creature, not a figment of the imagination, that corresponded to the brown bear *(Ursus arctus)*. After all, in an ancient Tibetan dialect, *yeti* translates as "snow bear." I hasten to add that this is an extraordinary animal—fearsome and preternaturally intelligent, as far as possible from the cuddly image people in the West sometimes have of bears.

These animals are nearly impossible to track, and for all their reality they remain deeply enigmatic. They avoid all contact with humans and are partly bipedal, nocturnal omnivores. Usually the males of the species, who roam from the group, are sighted.

The key to solving the yeti mystery lies not in separating the legend from a specific species of animal but in trying to connect two completely different modes of perception. Western visitors and mountain dwellers in these remote Himalayan regions have talked past each other for over a century, their divergent views of the yeti drifting ever further apart. And with the destruction of the world's wildernesses, we are losing the opportunity to appreciate those cultures whose view of life remains closely bound to nature—for that nature is disappearing. Whether Neanderthal or abominable snowman or brown bear or monster, the yeti lives in the opposition between civilization and wilderness.

I met the Dalai Lama on September 10, 1997, in South Tirol. We spoke about Kham—its handicrafts and the monasteries that are being rebuilt. "This is the second time in history that Tibetan culture has been resuscitated from Kham and Amdo," the Dalai Lama said in his quiet manner. We began talking of Tibet's wildlife: the takin, the wild donkey, the blue sheep—and the chemong.

"You know, we used to have chemongs in Norbulinka Park," the Dalai Lama said, laughing.

"Yes, there is a male and a female there now," I told him.

"Is this chemong such a strange animal?"

"Yes. A bear, and yet more than a bear."

"Isn't he like a grizzly bear?"

"That's what he looks like."

"And he abducts women?"

"That's what they say."

"That corresponds to the yeti legend," mused the Dalai Lama.

"Yes."

"Do you think that the migiö, chemong, and yeti might well be one and the same thing?"

"I not only think so, I am completely convinced that they are," I said. Then I put my finger to my lips, as did the Dalai Lama, as if acknowledging that this must remain our secret.

12

LIFE AND LEGEND

In his book *The Third Eye,* Lobsang Rampa, a self-proclaimed lama, describes an encounter he had with a yeti in a sort of heavenly oasis he claims exists in an unexplored part of northern Tibet's Chang Tang Desert:

> I was bending picking herbs, when something made me look up. There, within ten yards of me, was this creature that I had heard so much about. Parents in Tibet often threaten naughty children with "Behave yourself, or a yeti will get you!" Now, I thought, a yeti *had* got me. And I was not happy about it. We looked at each other, both of us frozen with fright for a period which seemed ageless. It was pointing a hand at me, and uttering a curious mewing noise like a kitten. The head seemed to have no frontal lobes, but it sloped

back almost directly from the very heavy brows. The chin receded greatly and the teeth were large and prominent. Yet the skull capacity appeared similar to that of modern man with the exception of the missing forehead. The hands and feet were large and splayed. The legs were bowed and the arms were much longer than normal. I observed that the creature walked on the outer side of the feet as humans do.[6]

Although I had never been to this part of Tibet, I knew immediately that what Lobsang Rampa recounts could not have happened. His descriptions of the landscape are also imaginary. Even in midsummer, when the snows recede to the distant boundaries of the mountain chains in the desert's most northern reaches, an icy wind blows through the rock formations. There are hot springs in the Chang Tang Desert, but not, as Lobsang Rampa claims, tropical plants. The valleys of the high plateau never turn green. Wildlife scampers away before you can tell if what you just saw was an antelope or a wild donkey.

Here is the back of the beyond, a place where even rumors lose their way. The powers of the imagination dissipate—as does Beijing's interest. The wilderness is empty.

As late as the 1970s, John Napier, a scientist specializing in primate anatomy, still believed that Neanderthals might have survived in this desert, managing to avoid extinction or assimilation into other species. But the Chang Tang Desert would have been no habitat for them. The question was, instead, could it be one for chemos? Many of the monks and local people believe that yetis roam these wide expanses.

True nomadic culture has disappeared from Sherpa country, but here, between the Trans-Himalayas and Kunlun, it still flourishes. Yak pastures can often be found at altitudes of eighteen thousand feet. The grass is so sparse that shepherds keep their flocks on the move, whistling, shouting, prodding, and throwing stones from morning till night. The animals need to be prevented from digging up the roots of the plants, and from becoming prey for wolves. Or perhaps yetis.

Day and night, summer and winter set the rhythm for the nomads, as they move their herds from one pasture to the next, bartering for grain, salt, and tea. They never till the soil. The Chang Tang Desert is no one's possession. The land once belonged to the monasteries or to feudal lords; now it belongs to the state—to the Chinese, in other words. But this desert—the highest in the world—is too large and inhospitable even for Tibet's masters, and the life of the yak nomads has changed little under Chinese rule. They are untouched by either communist or capitalist doctrine.

Their life is ruled by their yaks, which afford them everything they need to survive: their tents are woven of yak hair, their camps are carried from place to place by yaks, their campfires are stoked with yak dung, and the tea that they sacrifice to their gods before drinking is spiced with yak butter and salt.

In Tibet, every animal is considered sacred—and no animal can be slaughtered for any reason. That goes for the yeti, too. The Chinese conquerors have ignored Tibetan religion and continue to hunt wild animals, but they have not managed to eradicate them completely. During my travels I repeatedly saw wild donkeys, ibex, marmots, eagles, takins, owls, and wild yaks. Tibetans also consider the forests on which the wildlife depend for survival to be sacred. I spent a week traveling through the Chang Tang Desert and did not see a single tree. I understand why the Tibetans consider them sacred.

Poor as the Chang Tang Desert is in vegetation, it is rich in mineral resources. This does not augur well for its future. For centuries the superstitious nomads have not dared exploit the earth for fear of angering the earth spirits; the Chinese have no such fear. The local people gather at the borax-rich hot springs to collect salt crusts, which they use as a detergent, but would never try to extract the titanium or oil also to be found there.

It is here, in northern Tibet, and in the ravines of eastern Tibet, that most Tibetan legends originate, moving south with the nomads and getting embroidered upon with each step. In southern Tibet, where most of the Tibetans live in small villages, cultivating barley in the deep river valleys, these legends were turned into the myths gobbled up by outsiders like tales from another planet. For over two millennia Westerners have enveloped the "Land of the Snows" in mystery, a mystery that needed to be cultivated.

I ended my quest for the yeti in Mongolia, exploring the sprawling terrain between Kunlun and the Altai Mountains, where the sunlight shines more intensely than anywhere else in the world.

The Nazis, who viewed Central Asia as a sanctuary for a "proto-Aryan race," sought the remnants of a "Nordic spiritual aristocracy" there, while contemporary adventurers, who plan to use satellites to make thermographic scans of the entire Himalayan territory, seek undiscovered primates and legendary hominids—whose images, once captured, they will send around the globe via the Internet. They are not interested in the chemo, the animal upon which the mountain people have based the yeti legend. Finding a mere animal is not thrilling enough for these adventurers, and so they have pushed the yeti legend ever further into the realm of fantasy, ever further away from its true source. Yet they chase a legend—a phantom—with Land Rovers, airplanes, even with radio-controlled helicopters carrying camcorders.

To be fair, it is quite possible that mummified mammals corresponding to descriptions of the yeti might still be found buried in the arctic permafrost. And too little is known about the existence of cave bears in Central Asia (in Europe they became extinct during the last ice age) to pass final judgment on the origins of the yeti. Time will tell whether Neanderthal-like creatures, offshoots of the human genealogical tree, might have survived in the rugged mountains of Central Asia and Mongolia.

But one thing is certain: the Neanderthals' characteristics do not correspond to those of the yeti. All evidence points to a nocturnal species of brown bear ruling those icy terrains that during the day man believes are his. This bear can run, climb, and track far better than a man. It lives throughout Asia east of the Urals: from the taiga and the tundra all the way to the Bering Straits, as well as in Kamchatka, Sakhalin, Japan's Shantari Islands, Manchuria, Mongolia, Afghanistan, Persia, Syria, Palestine, Asia Minor, Kashmir, and the Punjab.

Because of the variety found within this species, people talk of bear populations and not of types of bear. Their behavior has not been sufficiently studied. As far as my research is concerned, so long as the legend of the yeti conforms to the reality of the dremo and the chemo and the chemong, genetic differences between these species are less significant than establishing differing behavior patterns or discovering a previously unknown species.

Scientists have stumbled upon new species in this century. The okapi, an African forest giraffe, was only discovered in 1900. The Chacoan peccary, a type of pig thought to have been extinct since the Pleistocene, was found in South America in 1972. In the early 1990s Vietnamese scientists discovered a new species of hooved animal. And in 1997, British scientists claimed to have found a previously unknown type of ape in the jungles of Sumatra. It walks upright. Recently, genetic testing has identified a species of Vietnamese ape as a separate primate.

Generally, however, we are killing off species far faster than discovering new ones. The few remaining orangutans are dying on the dusty gravel tracks of the Borneo jungles, or milling around villages, begging for food. Forest fires are destroying their habitat, and desperate animals invading rice paddies in search of food are killed by farmers. Had Indonesian conservationists not gathered the last of the orangutans into a rehabilitation center, they would now exist only in zoos.

The Tibetans have greater respect for living creatures. The Himalayan people have traditionally accorded the yeti a status higher than that of other animals—in some places, equal to humans—and so yetis have been left in peace. I hope that one day, once we have sufficiently studied these creatures, the question of whether they are cognizant will no longer be as important to us, and we will come to realize that like all animals they have the right to live in freedom and safety. And if we are truly wise, we will allow them to live in peace, as mountain people have done since time immemorial. That is in the end the only way to preserve the legend of the yeti.

The grizzly bears of North America are finding more and more supporters, and perhaps the realization that the yeti myth is a bear myth will encourage an awareness that radically differentiates between wilderness and zoo. Brown bears can survive in captivity as well as in the wilderness, but a bear in a zoo is a domestic animal. Only in the wild do these animals remind us that the Himalayas are a region in which humans do not belong.

Without wilderness there is no yeti. Thus, the survival of the yeti myth is dependent on the survival of the last wildernesses—areas so undeveloped that even the local population cannot conclusively confirm or refute the equation of the brown bear with the yeti. There is much more behind our thirst for monsters than curiosity or escapism. There is the fear that the earth is losing the last regions where myths can flourish.

Who can doubt the existence of the yeti? Many who have encountered the animal do not realize what they have seen, hence talk of mythical creatures. Those who have never encountered it—in other words, most people—allow themselves to drift into the realms of fantasy. In a time when resuscitated dinosaurs prowl our televisions, it matters little if the animals on the screen really exist. So long as people are certain these animals inhabit a land beyond the horizon, they willingly succumb to sensationalism. That is why "yeti footprints" will keep turning up throughout the Western world.

During my last expedition, an old nomad came to my tent. He aped my voice, then threw stones at me when I tried to get him to leave. "Yeti!" he shouted, making derogatory gestures and waving his hands at me, as if to shoo me away. Was he mad? Perhaps he was merely frightened. We eyed each other like animals. But from his expression and his gestures I could tell that he had heard about me, and that I would soon be a figure in the stories he would tell his grandchildren. A strange figure: "The man who kept asking everyone about the yeti, and who himself looked like one."

I did not want to know that tale, but I knew that it meant that the tale of the yeti—in some form—would exist forever.

Storytellers die; their stories live on.

NOTES

1. Slavomir Rawicz, *The Long Walk* (New York: The Lyons Press, 1997).
2. L. W. Davies, "Footsteps in the Snow," *The Alpine Journal* (published by Alpine Club, London) LXI, no. 293 (November 1956).
3. Edward W. Cronin, Jr., *The Arun: A Natural History of the World's Deepest Valley* (Boston: Houghton Mifflin Company, 1979).
4. Baird T. Spalding, *The Life and Teaching of the Masters of the Far East* (Los Angeles: DeVorss & Co. Publishers, 1937).
5. Nicholas Roerich, *The Heart of Asia* (New York: New Era Library, Roerich Museum Press, 1930, c. 1929).
6. T. Lobsang Rampa, *The Third Eye* (Brandt & Brandt, 1956/1958; reprint, New York: Ballantine Books, 1991).

WORKS MENTIONED
IN THE TEXT

Cronin, Edward W. *The Arun: A Natural History of the World's Deepest Valley.* Boston: Houghton Mifflin, 1979.

Davies, L. W. "Footsteps in the Snow." *The Alpine Journal* vol. LXI, no. 293 (November 1956).

Pliny the Elder. *Natural History.* Trans. Jones, W.H.S. Cambridge, MA: Harvard University Press, 1969.

Rampa, Lobsang T. *The Third Eye.* New York: Ballantine Books, 1991.

Rawicz, Slavomir. *The Long Walk.* New York: The Lyons Press, 1997; London: Constable, 1956.

Roerich, Nicholas. *The Heart of Asia.* New York: New Era Library, Roerich Museum Press, 1929.

Schäfer, Ernst. *Dach der Erde: Durch das Wunderland Hochtibet Tibetexpedition 1934/1936.* Berlin: Paul Parey, 1938.

Spalding, Baird T. *The Life and Teaching of the Masters of the Far East.* Los Angeles: DeVorss & Co. Publishers, 1937.

Waddell, L.A. *Lhasa and its Mysteries.* Mineola, NY: Dover, 1988.